I Ain't Doin' It

I Ain't Doin' It

UNFILTERED THOUGHTS FROM A
SARCASTIC SOUTHERN SWEETHEART

Heather Land

HOWARD BOOKS
New York   London   Toronto   Sydney   New Delhi

H Howard Books
An Imprint of Simon & Schuster, Inc.
1230 Avenue of the Americas
HOWARD
BOOKS New York, NY 10020

First Howard Books hardcover edition May 2019

HOWARD and colophon are trademarks of Simon & Schuster, Inc.

For information about special discounts for bulk purchases, please contact Simon & Schuster Special Sales at 1-866-506-1949 or business@simonandschuster.com.

The Simon & Schuster Speakers Bureau can bring authors to your live event. For more information or to book an event, contact the Simon & Schuster Speakers Bureau at 1-866-248-3049 or visit our website at www.simonspeakers.com.

Interior design by Davina Mock-Maniscalco

Manufactured in the United States of America

10   9   8   7   6   5   4   3   2   1

Library of Congress Cataloging-in-Publication Data

Names: Land, Heather, author.
Title: I ain't doin' it : unfiltered thoughts from a sarcastic southern
    sweetheart / by Heather Land.
Description: First Howard Books hardcover edition. | New York : Howard
Books, 2019. | "Howard Books fiction original hardcover."
Identifiers: LCCN 2018048357 (print) | LCCN 2018061380 (ebook) |
    ISBN 9781982104115 (eBook) | ISBN 9781982104092 |
    ISBN 9781982104092 (hardcover) | ISBN 9781982104115 (ebook)
Subjects: LCSH: Conduct of life—Humor. | American wit and humor.
Classification: LCC PN6231.C6142 (ebook) | LCC PN6231.C6142 L36
    2019 (print) | DDC 818/.602—dc23
LC record available at https://lccn.loc.gov/2018048357

ISBN 978-1-9821-0409-2
ISBN 978-1-9821-0411-5 (ebook)

This book is dedicated to every single one of you reading these pages. Laughter is medicine. May this ridiculous book be the Bengay to your aching joints.

To my children. I love you.
Be kind and love others. Never make fun of people (unless you have a filter on your face).

And finally, to my granny.
Jimmie Evangeline Cole
May 27, 1929–December 14, 2018
I wish you could've read this nonsense,
but you already knew all the stories anyway.

OH, THE PLACES YOU'LL GO . . .

"You have brains in your head. You have feet in your shoes. You can steer yourself any direction you choose. *(preferably the beach and/or Europe)*

"You'll look up and down streets. Look 'em over with care. About some you will say, 'I don't choose to go there.' *(true dat)*

"With your head full of brains and your shoes full of feet, you're too smart to go down any not-so-good street." *(one would think)*

Look, I really appreciate your insight there, Dr. Seuss. But apparently you don't have a booking agent who tells you where you're gonna be from week to week. And you've evidently never gone down any "not-so-good streets" on your early forties dating route (I ain't doin' it). We'll get to that in a later chapter (that could be its own book).

Yes, okay? I have brains in my head and some pretty

cute shoes, but some of the places on my journey I would most definitely not choose . . . have chosen. Whatever.

Here's the point. Some roads we go down are a little bumpy. They are not all newly paved, with an easy traffic flow and a steady pace of eighty miles per hour. Sometimes we even DO choose to go down the bumpy roads. Why? I don't know. That's why I'm in counseling. But listen, I can promise you this—some of the roads I've gone down were about as bad as I-40 into Arkansas, but some of the scenery has been breathtaking. Some of the people I picked up along the way (figuratively speaking) have made the biggest impact on my life. And those rocky roads have helped me appreciate the smell of fresh asphalt.

Sometimes we don't know where we're headed. We don't know what lies ahead. Most of the time it's a crapshoot. We take wrong turns here and there. But if we take time to breathe it all in, learn the hard lessons, and lean in to the ultimate Map Maker himself, we might actually enjoy the ride. We just might get to the other side and find that the risks were worth taking. We might even find out some things about ourselves on that ol' Arkansas stretch that we didn't know. We might find that the tears and the potholes actually made us a little more resilient—that we are weaker, but stronger, than we ever dreamed.

And maybe, just maybe, we'll learn to take a different route (date better guys) next time around. Maybe we'll learn that we are more than we ever thought we could be and that who we've become is more beautiful than who we were before. Maybe we'll find that we have a country-girl history but a big-city future.

When *I Ain't Doin' It* found its home, I was sitting behind a desk. I had just gone through another beautiful, ugly transitional time in my life—this time, a massive move with my kids, back home to live with my parents. I had taken a job just to get me back to Tennessee and over the hump, but it was a short hump and I needed stability.

Upon my resurfacing and transition back into "normal life," hilarity and sarcasm found their way back into my world as well. I had missed them like most people miss church during daylight savings. We finally had the band back together and I wasn't gonna let it breakup for anything ever again. This time, I was keeping all my members close and I was determined to climb back up the life chart once again. I was making a comeback.

Having mercy on myself in those coming days manifested in many different ways. Staying surrounded with people who loved me and held me accountable was crucial. Being good to myself in the form of mani/pedis and dinners with friends over talks and tears also helped. Reminding myself of who God says I am and combatting continual tapes that my brain was playing about how I wasn't worthy would also be a big part of my moving forward. And just as important a role in my healing process—laughter.

I've always had a knack for being able to make fun of myself, but after what I had been through, that would be a little slow-going. After a few months of recovery and my allowance to walk the process and start to heal, it didn't hurt quite like it did at first. It was so good to laugh again and find the funny in everyday life. Because as you know, life is funny and so are the people in it.

Now, I have a lot of good friends. Some of them get me more than others. The good ones are the ones who know all my faults and failures, know that I'm an idiot but love me just the same. The ones who get my humor, who understand the inner workings of my warped, sarcastic brain and appreciate all that it entails. And these friends are the select few that were getting the inside track on my nonsense coming straight at them on the daily . . . in the form of ridiculous videos. And hideous filtered videos of stupidity were how we coped with life and loss and nursing and pastoring and crunching numbers. It's how we coped with parent issues and children issues and painful issues. By laughing. And as if the tears weren't enough, the laughter kept us close and connected. Months had gone by when one day, a friend saw a video I'd sent just to her and our inner circle that particularly made her laugh. If I remember correctly, her exact words were, "You are so stupid . . . and these are really funny. You should post one on your page."

Umm . . . you just crossed the line. Post on social media?? NEVER! I am single but I don't want to stay that way forever, so no to that. No to public shaming. Have I not done that enough? Has my recent life choice not been enough public scrutiny for one person to have to endure?

A few weeks went by of more private nonsense and nudging to post between friends, until I finally said to myself, "What do you have to lose? Absolutely nothing." And with that, I posted a video to social media. And the funniest thing happened—people started to watch it. And they started to ask for more. More . . . I AIN'T DOIN' IT videos.

I looked at Abby and said, "What are they talking about, 'I AIN'T DOIN' IT'?"

"You said 'I AIN'T DOIN' IT' in your video." Hmm . . . So I did.

This, my friends, would prove to be the accident of all accidents—the phrase that would forever change the course of my life. And so with that request, and considering the fact that there is material on every corner, I made another video for public consumption and ended it with nothing other than I AIN'T DOIN' IT. People always ask, "Where do you get your material?" You're joking, right? Idiotic behavior and comical life situations are as readily available as Jesus' forgiveness upon repentance. That fruit is low hanging and ripe for the picking. You just say when.

After somewhere around video #3, a dear friend of mine, endearingly known as Whoa Susannah, asked if she could share my video on her page. "You'll need to start a fan page," she said.

"Umm . . . no," I said. A fan page? *Heck to the no. I ain't doin' it. I'm not trying to be somebody over here with these videos.*

Upon her persuasion that people are crazy, I decided to shield some of my private life from the outside world with what she said would be an influx of followers, and reluctantly started a fan page on the morning of Wednesday, September 6, 2017. By the time I went to church that night, 750 people already thought I was funny. *What?? That's crazy! So many people!* Off to church I went, only to refresh my page upon my return home to see 45,000. Then seven minutes later, 50,000. And so on and so forth.

I'll try to keep this part short. Just know that my world forever changed after that day. The next few weeks proved to be difficult as I tried to sort it all out. And sort WHAT out? What does this all even mean? My work was going so well, but I couldn't seem to concentrate as social media's response to my stupidity had me mesmerized. The numbers, they just kept going up. And people wanted more, so I would go sit outside in my car on my lunch break and make more dumb videos about nonsense. But nonsense, apparently, that the world was relating to, because day after day that beast kept getting bigger and bigger.

And while people laughed and commented and came back for more, I was healing. They say laughter is the best medicine, and I agree. I don't know about you, but I want to get where I'm headed (wherever that may be) with as much love, laughter, humility and confidence as I can possibly muster up, and live in enough freedom to share my ridiculous, shameful stories so others will be brave enough to tell theirs.

I'm talking to you.

Share your story.

Share the imperfections—the shame, the joy and the tragedy.

The good decisions and the bad.

Don't be afraid to tell people about your journey down Lovers' Lane and Psycho Path (been there).

I'm no counselor (unless you can earn credits by seeing one), but I would almost bet that as you share your stories and dig deep to find the humor buried in the rubble, you'll find your load getting lighter, your heart starting to heal and courage you didn't even know you had.

I hope this book of nonsense and bad judgment calls will help you laugh and love yourself again and not take life so dang seriously. Enjoy the ride. And don't be afraid of Arkansas. Joplin, Missouri, is way worse.

CHAPTER 1

SOUTHERN CHARM

The South—Tennessee, to be exact. Could there possibly be a more endearing place on the planet to grow up? The place where everyone says "Yes, sir" and "Bless her heart." Where sweet tea cures whatever ails you and where charm bracelets and monograms make up the DNA of women everywhere.

No. There could not be.

I mean, I, for one, question your salvation if you don't have a monogrammed handbag and at least twenty charms on your Pandora bracelet.

Who are you, even?

Oh, you don't have a monogrammed purse but you do have monogrammed boots.

I guess you're excused.

Monogrammed boots?!? WHAT, EVEN?!? Some of you reading this right now are asking the question—Is this even a thing?

Yes, my friend. Yes, it is. And it makes me want to die a thousand deaths.

Just last year, my friend at work sent me a picture over Snapchat of her new tennis shoes that she had monogrammed on the tongue. I swear on all things Southern, I dropped what I was doing, marched straight over to her office, phone in hand, opened her door, showed her the picture and said, "Umm . . . no." She laughed and said, "Umm . . . yes!"

The tongue?!?

Not the tongue!!!

Are we that bored? Do we really need to reinvent the monogram wheel? I mean, what difference does it make anyway? Do you think that if I see your mono-grammed koozie out at the ball field I'm going to look at those initials and say, "Oh, look. Brittney left her cup"?

NO!! I am still clueless as to who you are. The only thing I question is maybe your middle name. But who even cares?!

And why in Lord's name is it plastered on the back windshield of your car? This one gets me every stinkin' time! I am about as bewildered by this one as I am the lit-tle sticker-families on folks' back windows. Lady, you cannot even see out the back, your monogram is so big! WHY? Don't you know obscurity is the name of the game, girl? Remain a mystery! It's more exciting that way! Leave us something to wonder about. Good grief! Your monogram cleavage is hanging out there so big that you have left absolutely nothing to the imagination! Was that your goal? Is your giant window monogram the new low-cut V-neck? The daisy dukes of vehicle décor? If so, then well done. At least now we know exactly what kind of woman you are.

And you're not off the hook, men. Same goes for you and your giant business decals.

We see you!! Okay? We see that giant home you plastered across the back of your windshield, Smith Residential. And your phone number is so big I recited it all night in my sleep. We get the point.

(Insert eye-roll here.) The side of your truck just wouldn't do, would it? We get it. At least you had the decency to spell it out and not make us guess with a business monogram, I suppose. Before we know it, monograms will be the new identification code for Southern women—monogrammed tramp stamps to identify their bodies. What happens with those second and third marriages, huh? How exactly does that work? I'd love to know. I've lived in the South nearly my whole life, but the whole concept of monogramming still raises doubts in my head to this day. Never mind that monogram tattoo I got on my right wrist with my ex-husband's initial smack-dab in the middle. Don't you worry about that. This is about you, not me. At least I did mine with permanent ink on my body and not on the tongue of my shoes. (Dear God. What have I done?)

Look, sometimes you can escape it. Other times you drink the Kool-Aid. It was all I knew. Southern girl for life. A charm bracelet, though, I do not have. And I'm pretty sure I'm just about the only one. Women in the South love a good charm bracelet. At least this leaves just about zero work for you guys when it comes to gifts for major holidays. When in doubt, buy a charm. You don't know what could possibly be significant in her life right now? Just buy a heart. How can you go wrong there? Some women in the South have so many charms on their bracelets that you can either hear them coming a mile away or you could throw them into the pond a mile away and their bracelets would carry them all the way to the bottom and hold them there until the man of the family comes to their rescue in his really big jacked-up truck.

Is this just a Southern thing, too? I don't know, but I promise you this: I only dated one boy growing up who drove a car, and yes, I went out with more than one boy. All the other guys drove trucks. This was the norm where I come from. Never mind that these boys weighed a buck fifty sopping wet and their need for an extended cab was about the equivalent to me needing a new set of weights and a yoga mat. Although, there had to be someplace to house all their guns and waders, so I kind of get it. My dad never needed to worry about me ending up in the backseat of some ol' boy's truck. Not only because I was a good girl, but because it was never an option. Coolers are big and boots are muddy and guns are dangerous, and all these things covered the faded upholstery of their backseats. The front was the only place for me. There was literally no other room.

And did you know that boys in the South also love charm bracelets? Southern-boy charms are "purchased" upon the kill of a duck. The charms (also called duck identification rings) are located around the ankle of said duck, and upon death and removal, the charm is then placed as an extension of the Southern boy's duck call. Said duck-call charm bracelet is then hung on the rearview mirror and worn like a crown on the head. It is a symbol of manhood—of a good shot. The sign of victory—of his ability to conquer. For Christmas one year, I even bought my favorite boyfriend all things hunting, including a fourteen-karat-gold duck ring on a chain. He wore it proudly around his neck everywhere we went like it was an engagement ring. Looking back, I didn't even know I was proposing. I guess I should've gotten down on one knee, but he didn't seem to care. It was his favorite gift, second only to his new Remington box that I gave him to house all his shells. I am probably the best Southern girlfriend of all time. Listen and learn, fellow sisters. I've spent more money on hunting gifts over the years than I've probably spent on my own kids. Just a few years back, I bought my guy-at-the-time a new scope for his gun and new razors to skin his critters. More about deer hunting in another chapter. Just know, ladies, that when it comes to giving gifts to your Southern hunter-man, you will never run out of ideas.

Did you know that Southern boys who hunt are also good listeners? They are trained to be quiet, to listen for the limb to crack, for the duck to call, for the wings to flap. I always loved how my hunter-man seemed to listen so intently as I would empty out my soul and heart's deepest desires over a romantic catfish and hush-puppy dinner. I'm not sure if it was his training, his genuine love for me or the fact that repeated gunshots had created a temporary threshold shift in his ear canal resulting in hearing loss, but whatever the cause, he made me think he was listening. Well done, fella. Southern boys for the win!

And those catfish dinners would not be complete without at least a gallon of sweet tea.

"Would you like some tea with that sugar?"

This is how sweet tea is made in the South. My mama made it all during my growing-up years. Two cups of sugar to one pitcher and two tea bags. And I wondered why I was overweight till my junior year. It is a staple at the dinner table. It is such a given even when you eat out at restaurants that you have to intentionally ask for UNsweet tea. Otherwise, you will receive a giant glass of colored sugar-water with endless refills. Then you'll wonder why you're not hungry for dessert. It's because you just drank it.

"Eating out" is also a relative term in the South. We can do fine dining all day long, but sometimes when we say, "Let's go out to eat," we mean to the gas-station-turned-restaurant on the edge of town. Careful not to turn your nose up to these fine establishments. Clenny's has the best sausage and biscuits around. And summers at the lake afforded us the privilege of eating burgers at the corner grocery store on the daily. Best burgers on this side of Big Sandy.

See, when I was growing up, we practically lived at the lake during the summers. And living at the lake meant a few things for sure—tan legs, cutoff shorts and firing up the grill. If you're a Southern boy and you can't grill, I question your true heritage. You must've been born in the city and your mama just didn't tell you. Your daddy must not actually be your daddy. You'll have to hash that out in counseling. I just know that it's on my list. You know "the list," girls—the THINGS I'M LOOKING FOR IN A MAN list. Right along with a possible short-trimmed beard and an ability to go from rugged to classy faster than you can say "Hey, y'all!"

Southern lingo is its own thing, too, in case you didn't know. Apparently, I have a bit of a drawl, myself.

And just in case the phrase "I ain't doin' it" didn't give it away, I am partial to a few other favorites that seem to follow me everywhere I go, as well. It doesn't matter if I'm drinking coffee in the Midwest or sipping tea in London, I will never be able to shake the faulty, unconventional articulation that spews from my mouth like soybeans from a deer gut. To some it's endearing; to others, appalling. I get it. No offense taken. Sometimes I can dial it back to at least sound like I graduated high school. Other times it is as obvious as the monogram on your back windshield.

"Y'all," for example, is a phrase that I will never be able to shake. To actually divide this contraction would be like taking the sugar out of tea, and what God has joined together, let no man put asunder (Holy Bible).

"Holler" is another one of my personal favorites. "Holler at me." It's simple—self-explanatory. And listen here, Urban Dictionary, "holler" was around long before "holla" (which I also use). Never mind. We have more words that will forever and always be ours and not yours, general public. You can try and take the word out of the South, but you will never be able to take the South out of the word.

Like, "fixin.'" Oh, Lord, yes. This is my go-to. I don't mean to do it. It's just engrained into my knower like the alphabet. I can't unhear it. I can't unknow it. Just like that one time when that little boy wet his pants sitting beside me in Mrs. Harrison's second-grade class. I felt so sorry for him. I will never not remember his face, his name, his shame. I will never be able to unsee that, or un-smell it, for that matter. It's forever a part of my makeup. I digress . . .

"I'm fixin' to." Fixin' to what?

ANYTHING!

You can be "fixin' to" just about anything you want. "Fixin'" and "fixin' TO" are TWO different things, just so you know. I ain't "fixin'" anything. Let's get that straight right now. I'm not handy. That's what boys are for. But I'm "fixin' to" run to the store. You wanna go? I don't see the problem here. Southerners get made fun of so much for this. It's as normal as Canadians saying "a boot" when they're really trying to say "about." It's as normal as a lift kit on a Chevy. But that's a whole nother story.

A "whole nother." What even? I don't know, but I say it. It just feels abso-stinkin'-lutely right to divide a word with a whole nother word. Doesn't that feel right to you? No? Hmm . . .

Well, you just don't know how to speak Southern then.

Bless your heart . . .

Oh, the good ol' "bless your heart." This phrase has multiple meanings to exemplify the many personalities of the true Southern woman. This phrase is about as backhanded and sarcastic as they come, but it can also be used in the most genuine sense of the word, depending on the occasion. Now, there ARE some Southern women out there who are soulless, who can cut you to the bone if you step over onto their side of the tracks, talk to their man, take their parking spot. But most Southern women have some sort of chip reader that was dug deep into their skin at birth that really can sincerely tap into the feels of other women. It's called empathy. But make no mistake—if we don't have it, we can at least make you think we do.

"He walked right out and left you? Bless your heart . . ."

You don't know, do you? You don't know if I mean it or if I'm secretly thinking that you deserved it. You don't know and you never will.

"You mean you got arrested for beating the crap out of your boyfriend's wife, but it was self-defense? Bless your heart . . ."

Still don't know, do you? You don't know if I'm on Team Mistress or Team Boyfriend's Wife (yes—that one).

And you'll never know, bless your heart. Because being a Southern woman means we don't necessarily want to hurt your feelings unless abso-stinkin'-lutely necessary, but make no mistake that we can if we need to. We are fierce, cunning, smart and sly. We can bless your heart but trip you walking down the runway of the Miss Milan No-Till Pageant so fast you won't know what hit you. Because you see, we Southern women know our pageants. Don't we, gals?

Pageants are as common as fried okra where I'm from. They are a public form of Southern entertainment intended to celebrate beauty and poise, talent and grace. But let's get real—just as often, we end up with tumbles and tears and missed notes and "I'm just not pretty enough" to the point that we could've taken the money we spent on all that hair spray and those tap shoes and bought a lifetime supply of "who gives a crap."

I just made some enemies. Look, it's fine if you're a pageant girl. One of my best friends growing up was a pageant queen. I used to fix her hair for her pageants, okay? I'm not hating on your extracurricular activity. I'm just saying that sometimes we are more concerned with the bathing suit and heels and not concerned enough that Miss Sunny Side Up can't even read her fishbowl question.

I'm not throwing stones, okay? I mean, how can I?

I was in Miss Milan No-Till.

The year was 1997. I was twenty years old and dating a hometown boy. He had the best family in all the world, which included twin sisters and a mother who still feels like my own. I loved them and they loved me and bless their hearts, they thought it was a good idea to con me into entering our hometown pageant. A pageant representing my city's adoption of the no-till production of crop growth—a method of farming where the soil is left undisturbed between the harvest of one crop and the planting of another (yes, I googled that).

I mean, it's kind of a big deal, though. Who wouldn't want to be the No-Till Queen? You could get all the way to Miss Tennessee and probably even get your chance at having your picture displayed on a tractor or something cool like that. I figured I should give it a go. Plus, if my people were saying I could do it, they had to be right.

"It's a scholarship pageant," they said.

"It's easy," they said.

"You can do it," they said.

"All you have to do is put on this dress that we will pay for ourselves, and you may have to just answer a question or two, but that's it."

Well, how hard could that be? Okay, then.

I wasn't really pageant material, but I was fairly cute, and I could put my hand on my hip and walk a straight line. Knowing that I had no other means of paying for my schooling and nothing to lose but my dignity, I decided this could potentially be achievable.

What started as a simple yes, then turned into weeks upon weeks of intense preparation for Dirt Day.

We rented a dress, then another dress, then bought

makeup and pantyhose and hair spray and we even bought a suit because, "Oh hey! Guess what? You have to go through an interview process with a panel of judges but you are gonna do GREAT!!" And then we bought a cassette tape with music to accompany me as I sang in the talent portion of the contest.

And then the day came.

I will never forget.

My heart races and all the blood drains from my face even as I type this. My sensory nerves remember and they send signals to my central nervous system right this very minute as if I'm reliving that nightmare all over again. The nightmare where I was awake and had to wear a . . .

BATHING SUIT!!!! (Southern for "swimsuit.")

WHAT?!? No freaking way am I wearing a bathing suit with pantyhose and heels on a stage in front of hundreds of people, maybe everybody in my whole town!! No. No. No.

It's hard enough for me to wear one at the lake!

I sadly withdraw my name from consideration.

I'm sorry, but I must remove my name from the ballot.

I regret to inform you that I will no longer be running for Miss Milan No-Till. I have suddenly come down with a case of "You have got to be smoking crack to think I am wearing a bathing suit on a stage."

I sincerely hope I have not thrown off the lady who is

making the sparkly numbers for us to pin to the outside of our garments. Tell her I'm sorry and that I'll reimburse her for the glitter.

Red welts covered my chest and neck when Mama Bear told me the news. Trapped in the car with nowhere to jump out, I had to sit and listen to all the reasons I could and would, in fact, wear the bathing suit and do the thing. She was smart to tell me while we were in a moving vehicle on the way to the wherever-you-go-to-rent-pageant-bathing-suits, because she knew I would be outta there faster than you could say "Contestant #3."

Somehow, some way, I calmed down and even found a royal-blue one-piece that not only covered most of my parts, but really made my eyes pop. And it looked killer with those nude heels.

We were back in business.

Judgment Day was finally here. I had won Miss Milan Tiny-Tot when I was five, and I beat out a lot of girls to do it. Surely this would be a piece of cake. And if possible, maybe I could even eat a piece of cake when it was over, because I was starving. My friend Emily had also gotten talked into drinking the Kool-Aid, so having her by my side would be my consolation should I walk away empty-handed.

This was an all-day event. I was like a bride preparing for her wedding day, but with a lot of other brides, and with only the possibility of a groom. We were all preparing ourselves like Esther for the king (Holy Bible), but only one of us would get the honeymoon.

Well, I didn't win the groom, but I am pleased to announce that not only did I make it down the runway in my gorgeous white evening gown, strut my stuff in my royal-blue bathing suit, sing my song to perfection and tell the whole town how I planned to end world hunger, but I also walked away with the second-place title and a $400 scholarship to my local community college—which I cashed in that very next semester for fourteen hours of music courses.

I may not have taken home the title of Miss Milan No-Till, but I did walk away with a trophy and a scholarship, a really proud squad and some really great material for that one time that I wrote this book called *I AIN'T DOIN' IT*. I grabbed myself a milk shake on the way home, then made myself a hot bath and an inner vow that I would never grace the runway again. I know a lot of people out there are shocked and disappointed, but I plan on keeping my promise.

I'm sure the remains of anything we purchased for the pageant were sold in some yard sale years later. I think that's a Southern thing, too. When I lived in Colorado Springs we had garage sales, and we even had neighborhood garage sales. In the South, though, we don't really care about preparation, or about keeping it a surprise—keeping it under wraps till the big day. We aren't at all concerned about getting our junk stolen or protecting it from wind, rain or animals. We also believe in keeping the whole experience purely authentic, meaning if we decide that we are broke or sick of all our junk, we will not hesitate to throw that mess on the front lawn at any given moment without the fair warning of a yard sale sign tacked onto the nearest light pole.

"I'm sick of this couch."

Done. Name your price. What would YOU give for a twenty-year-old, sunken pleather couch with three legs missing? Never mind that, because we will throw in the books we've been using to prop it up for free. We have no shame. Social media is even taking a liking to yard sales. A girl I know put some colostomy bags up on the Facebook yard sale and sold them for a pretty penny. I hear that these are expensive and as long as they're unused, this would be the place to buy your bags. Still, though, I'm sticking with a solid no on this. On the flip side, probably nobody is going to be asking you where you got your colostomy bag. Your Louis Vuitton bag? Yes. But not your colostomy bag.

This mirrors the likes of selling your used underwear at a yard sale. You just don't do that. Except that in the South, people do. There is no limitation on the items you can deem as sale-worthy.

Half-used bottles of salad dressing.

Christmas lights that don't work.

A taxidermy squirrel.

People will buy just about anything.

Sometimes our Southern yard sales prove to be a pretty lucrative side gig. I once made $600 at a yard sale, only to find out later that I accidently sold a box full of all my children's homemade Christmas ornaments. I cried and told myself "You can't take it with you when you go," but I was devastated. And what kind of person doesn't return that sort of thing? If you or someone you know hangs my daughter's homemade Rudolph ornament made out of an egg carton or a picture of my son in a beaded wreath on your Christmas tree every year and you are reading this right now, shame on you. I'm going to be praying for you (not really). That's for another chapter. Still, I don't know how you sleep at night. Probably very well, since I think I also sold you a top-of-the-line mattress for about $20.

Whatever. At least I made a little cash to help buy Halloween costumes and all the mess my kids had to have for school that fall. And at least we got in one final sale before it turned off cold. ("Turned off"—not only used to describe my current state of being regarding disgusting men, but also used to replace the word "got," as in "It suddenly got cold"—"It suddenly turned off cold.")

And what also happens during prime yard sale season? Lawn-mowing.

Now, this may not be a regional or geographical phe-nomenon. Maybe other gals partake in this aggressive act of servanthood as well, but I can tell you with certainty that women in the South love to mow yards. Some women. Not all. Mostly all, but what I'm trying to say is, NOT ME.

My mother is an avid lover of mowing lawns. It's somehow some sick form of therapy for her mind, body and soul. She will get out there and nearly stroke out from the heat, but come in satisfied. I will never under-stand it. I have mowed a yard a grand total of zero times, and I plan on continuing my run until I draw my last breath. Beat that streak, Snapchat. If my only accom-plishment in life is that I never mowed a yard, I will con-sider it a victory on my deathbed. I would rather cut my nails with hedge clippers for the rest of forever than cut grass.

I AIN'T DOIN' IT.

Although, my mother does always get a nice tan—that other thing that Southern women love to do.

My mama introduced me to the tanning bed at the ripe old age of thirteen. Tanning beds were just making a splash and I was curious, but I was scared. I didn't want to lie in that coffin, but I didn't want to remain milky white, either. Why? I don't know, because girls who work the Paris runway are whiter than the driven snow, but in my teenage years, having a tan was where it was at. So I went, and I got hooked. And I tanned the life outta my skin well into my twenties. Not only did I get in the beds, but I moved away to Florida for my college years and stayed lobster red for about nine months out of the year. I am reformed and try to take care of my skin nowadays, but in the South, I can always tell who lies in a tanning bed, nay, OWNS a tanning bed, and who doesn't. I almost put my wallet and car keys in a lady's mouth at Walmart one day thinking it was my leather purse. She was standing *way* too close.

I have put my roots down in other parts of the country. I have made other states my home at various times throughout the years and I may do so again, but at the end of the day, I still hang my hat in Tennessee. At the end of the day I am still a Southern girl. I may not mow yards and monogram my car, and I may not have a Pandora bracelet that could put the hurt on Floyd Mayweather, but I am Southern through and through. I may secretly wish that a British man would come and sweep me off my feet and take me to London to live in his flat, but the truth is, a good ol' Southern boy is just fine, too. Nothing beats a burger from the gas station and a good ol' worn-in purse from a yard sale (but seriously, y'all, if you've seen my Christmas ornaments, holler at me).

The South is special, and not in a "bless its heart" kind of way. It's nostalgic. It's hot dogs and the ball field and team spirit. It's monograms and sweet tea and country music. It's my people, my heritage. It's hospitality on a whole nother level. If "I AIN'T DOIN' IT" was a geographical location, it would most definitely be the South. It's home, and with all its mosquitos and imperfections, it's abso-stinkin'-lutely perfect.

CHAPTER 2

RED IS YOUR COLOR

*M*ost of the places I have the pleasure of visiting offer at least a little something in the way of excitement. A new five-star restaurant, interesting people, rib eyes on sale at the Dollar Tree. But ALL of them lend their hand at providing me with new material. Like that one place in Arkansas that was known for their fancy bologna (two words that should never be put in the same sentence). Or that one place tucked up in the foothills of Virginia that had no retail establishments but tons of storage buildings and billboards advertising basement space. I thought we were driving onto the set of *Deliverance*. I kept listening for the banjos and I kept my eye on all the toothless men, but we made it out alive. One thing that I can usually count on anywhere I go—somewhere within a twenty-mile radius there is a Walmart.

For some, Walmart is nightlife. For others, it's an all-day shopping adventure. "Hey, Karen. Call the girls. Let's make a day of it." I mean, why not? Where else can you get a week's worth of groceries, a bed-in-a-bag, dog food and makeup, all for under $100? Who needs Sephora anyway? (Me, that's who.)

Don't think for one second that my hard-earned money hasn't kept those doors open for a solid fifteen years. I've got more Walmart lip gloss than you can shake a stick at. And I've been to my fair share of bachelorette parties, but I promise you this—I've watched my children stuff more ones into that claw machine than I've ever seen stuffed into . . . I digress.

What I want to know is this—where are the Walmart workers hiding out when you need them? Are they in the back playing with fidget spinners? Are they in the stockroom trying on the Halloween costumes or back in the photo lab checking out what you did last Saturday night? I'll never know, because when I need them most they're nowhere to be found. That place can be at max capacity looking like a stinkin' tornado shelter, but guess how many lanes are open?

One.

Just one.

"The one" is always in the center of the store, and the line is always backed up into the pajamas.

"The one" does, however, create lovely opportunities to meet new people. Once I was in "the one" for so long that we held a camp meeting. Somebody preached, we sang hymns and three people committed their lives to the Lord. We're lucky we were at Walmart, because we just shook up a Sprite and went ahead and baptized them all right there while we waited.

It was a beautiful experience. Almost as beautiful as the time I was in there so long I delivered a baby. Right there in the line. We got there when the woman was about four months pregnant and finally were able to check out a few hours after her delivery. Lamaze was probably my favorite part, but watching the head crown was pretty epic as well. This paragraph is full of lies and nonsense, but it's how I feel every time I'm in the line— like it's never going to end. Like I'm never going to see my children again—only other people's children, whom I grow to despise with every passing second. Can't you shut that kid up, ma'am? Good grief!! No wonder you're wearing your pajamas in public. That kid is so loud I don't even know how you can hear yourself think!

Not only does Walmart provide us with tons of life experience and the basic necessities of life (toilet paper and nail polish), it also provides us with hours of entertainment. I mean, "the people of Walmart" have their own dedicated website, for crying out loud. And I swear some of them are straight outta my hometown.

On one of my recent outings, I came across something that not only raised questions in my mind, but the hair on the back of my neck. Right as I turned the corner from picking up some $1.29 Suave shampoo and conditioner for the kiddies, there she was. Let's call her Betty Jo. She was every bit of sixty-two, with each and every day of that rode-hard life spent in the tanning bed for a daily minimum of sixty-two minutes. It was apparent to me that she was preparing for a night out on the town. One problem, though—she just couldn't quite get settled on her preferred shade of red. How do I know? Because I stood there in jaw-dropping horror for what felt like sixty-two years as I watched her try on every shade Cover Girl had to offer. By the time every stick on the color wheel had touched her crusty, charred lips there was a whole group of us gathered 'round. I tried to hide my reaction, but in case you didn't know, disguising my feelings is not one of my strong suits.

The look on my face could only stand in comparison to the same one I must've had when I learned that my ex put a hot tub in his front yard right after my departure (missed it by the skin of my teeth). And this wasn't just any hot tub. It was an inflatable that was barricaded from the outside world by a homemade gazebo. This designated wet-party-room was decorated like a war hero. It didn't have a purple heart pinned on its chest, but it did have about sixty-two purple strobe lights pinned up around it. And don't forget the TV trays—they flanked its sides like somebody had issued a call to arms. When I learned of this vile act that was being committed against everyone who ever drove down that street after dark, I dropped to my knees and gave thanks to my Lord and Savior for delivering me from a life of redneckery and what would've been an absolute handing-over of my dignity. If I ever doubted it before, I knew right then—Jesus saves.

I digress . . .

Back to the subject at hand.

As I watched Betty Jo continue to narrow down her choices, I couldn't help but wonder . . . where exactly have her lips been? You know what? Scratch that. I don't wanna know. But I *would* like to know how in Lord's name you can, in good conscience, touch that merch to your mouth, knowing you just sucked down a tuna sandwich, and walk off like nothing ever happened. And I would also like to know how that date worked out. Was he happy with your color choice? Did he feel like he had his own real-life cover girl? Holler at me when it's over and give me the deets. I'll be at home drowning out your memory and scrubbing my lips with a pumice stone. Also, remind me to cancel my membership to the tanning bed. And cheers to you, Betty Jo.

You may be gone, but try as I might, you'll never be forgotten.

Moving on . . .

I feel like for the most part I've been a pretty good kid most of my life. I never gave my parents any trouble, except for that one time I lied and told them I was spending the night with a friend but got caught going dancing with my high school boyfriend instead. I've always tried to make good choices, be kind to people and, generally speaking, "do the right thing." So, why, every time I get in line at Walmart, do I get stuck with the checkout lady who talks about every single purchase I'm making and keeps me there for a thousand years? What did I do to deserve this, Lord? Have I not paid my penance?

I have run into every single person I don't like from church and I spoke to every single one. I took a different route when the long-lost family of fifteen congregated for a meet-'n'-greet in the noodle aisle. I helped a (perfectly capable) lady in her motorized scooter reach the bottled water on the top shelf, and I took a cussing when I accidentally clipped the heels of the man who stopped his buggy right in front of me. Why, then, must I always be punished by the checkout lady when it comes time to check out?

"These avocados sure are ripe."

"I didn't know *Fixer Upper* was in its last season."

"Hmm . . . it's your time of the month, huh?"

Okay, that's it!! Jesus, take the wheel! By the time it's over I'm about ready to throw in a box of Marlboro and a three-pack of lighters for the win. I'll learn on the way home. Good grief!

Ma'am, I love that you're an extrovert, okay? We can

go have a coffee later, but right now I'd really just love to get home before my youngest graduates high school. Is this too much to ask? No. It's really not. Now, slide that junk across that belt so I can leave. I've got a life to live.

I don't know about you, but by the time I get to the checkout line I GOTS TO GO! Get me out that door so I can go call my counselor. How soon can you get me in? I have just heard enough incorrect grammar to make my ears bleed. I have also learned that SpongeBob sleep pants are, in fact, no longer used just for sleeping, and I've taken an internal oath to learn how to make my own lipstick. Buy me a goat and some food coloring. Whatever. I don't care. Just help me process today's events so I can go back to being a functioning adult. And hey, counselor, can you add this one to the list? You'll never believe what I just seent with my own I's.

Right there, less than two feet in front of me, I watched the making of my very first horror film. I observed intently as a lady removed everything but the kitchen sink from her bra, only to finally locate in its deepest, darkest depths her sweaty money. My eye sockets, while traumatized, could not peel away.

Show me more. No, what?!? Stop!! Gross!

I can't take it!

How are you doing that? Is this a magic trick?

Everybody gather 'round!

Are you gonna pull a rabbit outta your bra? Hey, by

the way, if you know any card tricks I'd love to impress my kids over dinner if you've got a few more minutes.

Also, I feel like carrying pictures of your grandkids in your bra is a little nasty, but whatever, ma'am. Maybe that's just me.

Hey, quick question. Do you ever hear these items in your bra crying out for help? Can they breathe down there? 'Cuz you got that mess locked down like Shawshank, lady! I'm pretty sure I just saw Morgan Freeman jump out from between your cleavage.

Oh my gosh, is that a flask? Will you share? 'Cuz I feel like I need it to get through whatever's coming next. Do you have any saline down in there? My eyes need a bath!

Ma'am, I hate to interrupt the show, but one request. Could you please be careful and only pull out things that are unattached to your body? I feel like this is an accident waiting to happen.

Thankfully, being the seasoned magician she was, only tangible items were removed from the nook and cranny of all nooks and crannies. But why, though? I don't know and I never asked. I just know this: if the only action that lady ever gets is from the plethora of goodies she deposits in her own cleavage, she will never go unsatisfied another day in her life. As for me, I ain't doin' it.

As you well know, the world is crawling with all

kinds. Most of these "kinds" can be found at Walmart, but regardless, you will not have to look far to find the people who grate your nerves like sharp cheddar and shock you harder than the Kardashians. It doesn't matter if I'm in the Walmart line or at the bank. They are everywhere and they are on me like flies on stink. And I want to roll my eyes and huff until the mirrors in the makeup aisle fog. But every stinkin' time I always feel it. Well, not always—sometimes I feel rage, disgust and awe, but often I feel it—conviction. Then grace. The Lord has such a sweet way about Him. He has a voice that says, "You don't know what the checkout lady goes through, Heather. You don't know what kind of day she's had. Ask her (*Oh, please God, no*). Maybe you're the first person who has smiled at her today. Ask the bra lady if you can see the pictures of her grandkids (*No thanks, God*).

Noooo!!!! Jesus, please leave me alone and just let me roll my eyes and huff so the people across the street can hear me. I'll feel so much better.

Then there He is again, reminding me it's not about me.

One of my closest friends, Abby, is a nurse. She is genuinely one of the sweetest people I've ever known. Recently, one of her patients threw her bedpan on the floor and laughed as she had to clean it up. Now look, my girl is human, okay? She wasn't particularly thrilled with having to wipe up this lady's disgusting bodily fluids as she was being mocked. She went to The School of Sar-

casm like some of the rest of us, and if I know her, she
was having to lock it down pretty tight. But you know
what? Her love for Jesus and for this lady overruled any
frustration she was feeling. And she would do it all over
again just to get to show that lady the love of Christ,
which is what she did. Because it's what she's called to
do. It's what we're all called to do.

Now, I'm not suggesting we be doormats all in the
name of Christianity. Sometimes we have to stand up and
speak out and say, "Do you mind NOT throwing your
(extremely full) bedpan at me? Many thanks," or,
"Ma'am, I am so sorry, but I am in the hurry of a lifetime." Hopefully, we'll have the grace to know the whens
and hows. It is so hard. I know . . .

But here's the truth. I have to confess it: sometimes I
get so wrapped up in my hatred for ridiculous behavior,
and my need for dumb people to get away from me, that
I forget to check my attitude at the door. Here's the other
truth: we never know what people go through. We never
know what they face when they go home. I mean, have
you seen some of these faces? (That was uncalled for.) I
mean, seriously, though. Betty Jo could've had a really
strenuous morning at the tanning bed. We don't know.

I forget sometimes that there are people all around
me who are doing hard things in life and who are sick
and grieving and crying on the inside. I forget that I'm
not the only one who has issues. I forget that sometimes

our troubles make us angry and cranky and that nobody gets THAT upset over how far back the Walmart line is backed up. We act out of character sometimes when life pins us up against the wall. I know firsthand. There is always more to the story.

Sometimes I miss the mark. Sometimes I roll my eyes and huff my breath until somebody catches me, but I'm trying really hard to be salt and light. I'm trying to relate and understand and ask the checkout lady how her day has been. I've cried my way through the aisles of stores more times than I can count, dealing with what life and the precious people in it were throwing my way. I know what it's like to need the smile. I know what it's like to be struggling and need understanding. I cannot say that I know what it's like to pack my bra full of snacks for the road or touch lipsticks to my parts and set them back in good conscience for the next unsuspecting soul to use. I do, however, know what it's like to be human. So, next time you're in Walmart and that checkout lady starts to look through your magazine, smile, make a joke and keep it moving. Grab a tube of lipstick (I ain't doin' it) and hit the door. Let Walmart make you better, not bitter. Grab your sanity and a Sprite and move along. And when you see Betty Jo out tonight, tell her red is her color.

CHAPTER 3

TRAVELING MERCIES

W hy, when you are about to leave for a trip, do the people around you always pray for traveling mercies? "Lord, be with her and give her traveling mercies." Have I already done something wrong on this trip and somehow you telepathically know about it? Please fill me in so I won't do the thing. Are you a prophet? Am I going somewhere I shouldn't? Am I going to dip, drink, cuss, smoke or chew or hang out with boys that do? What?? Tell me!!! The suspense is killing me!

I've never understood this phrase . . . until now.

I've always loved to travel. Even as a little girl I loved road trips. My parents weren't exactly world travelers, unless you consider going to the lake traveling the world (which I don't). I was always looking for opportunities to get out of town. My senior trip to the Bahamas was a great introduction to a different culture, but I wanted to go other places, too, where I didn't feel pressure to let people I didn't know put tiny dookie braids in my hair. So, when I went off to college (before I dropped out) I joined a choir that I knew traveled religiously. I longed for something beyond the small-town life I'd always known. I always knew somewhere deep in my knower that one day I would travel the world and experience all the things—see the sights, live on the edge. And by "live on the edge" I mean go to London, sip tea, shop and visit the queen's castle.

When this whole crazy *I AIN'T DOIN' IT* train started rolling and travel became a part of daily life, I was on board (see what I did there?). Where do I sign?

Yes to travel.

Yes to going and doing and seeing and eating and drinking and all the things.

Yes, yes, yes. When do we leave for Europe?

Wait, what?

Hold the phone. What did you say?

Missouri?

Hmm . . . well, okay. I'm up for Missouri. There are people there that I haven't met, experiences that I haven't had. Although, I've been to the Arch and to a Cardinals game already.

But . . . well, still. Okay. Let's go.

Where in Missouri? Joplin? Isn't there a scripture about that place? Can anything good come from Joplin? Wait, no. That's Nazareth. Okay, whatever. Joplin it is.

Now, let me say this—the people we experienced in Joplin were the best! I spoke at a conference for an entire weekend and the fine folks of that area were nothing short of wonderful. But Joplin . . . I ain't gonna lie. Your city is a little weird.

No disrespect.

I have never seen so many retail establishments (with so many weird names) crammed into a single square mile in all my life. Goodness gracious alive! Between Tennessee and Missouri there was nothing but five million miles and five million cattle. I was convinced y'all were all a bunch of cow milkers. But then there it was—an endless array of job opportunities waiting to be had. Right there on the strip. If you or someone you know needs work, send them to Joplin.

Maybe you're a baker of sorts but a regular ol' bakery just isn't cutting it for you anymore. Then how about a bakery outlet? Look, I know what an outlet is, okay? It cuts out the middleman. Please don't write me letters schooling me on the definition. But let's get real. I don't know about you, but when I go outlet shopping I'm fairly certain that I'm gonna find last season's open-toe shoes, maybe some home décor items that have been banged up in transit. So, then, what in the world do you suppose is at this bakery outlet?

Bread that didn't rise?

Jelly donuts with no jelly?

Honey buns, no honey?

Last month's muffins?

I promise you, if I had driven by during business hours I would have you some answers. Please go there and find out for me. But don't bring me any unleavened bread or sugarless cupcakes. Bring me a reason this store is in business.

If you're an orthodontist, maybe you'd like to work at UNCOMMON ORTHODONTICS. I mean, that sounds totally normal, doesn't it? Maybe I'm just small-minded, but why, exactly, do we need orthodontics to be uncommon? Some things need to be common. Like the sense of whoever named UNCOMMON ORTHODON-TICS. I appreciate you trying to be all cutting edge, but if I'm going to the ortho for braces on my teeth, I don't want to walk out with braces on my legs. Can I get an amen? Risk it if you want. I would rather brush my teeth with one of those giant toothbrushes they brought to elementary school for demonstration every single day for the rest of my life than go to UO. I ain't doin' it.

Let me tell you what I did do, though. There is something you need to know about this one place. Brace yourself. It's not as innocent as it sounds. And just know, if you choose to go in and apply, there's a great chance your mother and your pastor will know it, and it ain't something you're gonna want on your résumé. Proceed with caution.

The store?

BRITTNEY'S TOY BOX.

As we drove into town, there she was. Brittney. Right there two steps from a major intersection smack-dab in the middle of town. I said to my longtime-friend-turned-assistant, Tosha, "Hey, look. A toy store. Let's stop off and get the kids a few things before we head back to Tennessee."

As I began looking around, I felt like their broad selection of "toys" covered every possible scenario you could think of and some that my brain just wouldn't let me consider, but none of these "toys" seemed to be what I would call child-friendly. It took me a solid sixty seconds before my face turned fifty shades of red and I realized . . . *Oh crap. This is a giant toy box filled with prizes for dirty grown-ups, not children coming out of the dentist.*

Still, I couldn't look away. My stomach turned at the thoughts swirling in my head, but the questions in my mind wouldn't turn me loose.

"Lord, I'm sorry I'm in here. I just came in for a stuffed rabbit and an Xbox card. And I'm also sorry that Brittney isn't smart enough to hide this big, giant toy box off of an exit like most of 'em do. And I'm sorry her business isn't making enough money for her to tint these windows. Do you want me to give her some money, God? It can be my offering."

As the weirdness in my mind kept unfolding, I finally got the mental fortitude to find the exit and leave (empty-handed). I went back to the hotel, pulled out a makeup wipe and began scrubbing the white off of my skin in the hopes that it would penetrate my forehead and seep into the memory part of my brain and wipe all the vivid pictures and dirty thoughts away (no luck).

"Lord, forgive me. I didn't even do anything wrong, but I feel like I just took a bath in cow manure. Please give Brittney some tint money. You did a great job blessing her with a very creative, manipulative way to get mothers to come into her store, but maybe you could drop it in her heart to carry a children's line of a more innocent nature for those of us who wander in, in search of stuffed animals and baby dolls. And have mercy on me as I venture off into the next town full of toy boxes. Yes, have mercy. Traveling mercies."

Now I know what they meant. They should've prayed harder.

My travels have me moving across the country on a weekly basis. I go from small town to big city in a single afternoon, and I love them both just the same. But let me tell you about my favorite place to be.

When you walk in the front door, the smell of something that got stuck in the toaster fills the air. Dishes fill the sink and scuff marks from Lord only knows what stain the once-white walls. Shoes are on the living room floor along with candy wrappers and chip bags. Beds are unmade and thermostats are adjusted to either blazing hot or freezing cold. And the sound of my little people's voices fills up the air so sweetly that nothing compares.

It is home.

All of the places I go and all of the people I meet pale in comparison to the boy and the girl who live in my home and call me Mama. There is no city entertaining enough, no concert hall grand enough, to make me forget where my heart lies. They are the real adventure. My children remind me daily that no matter where life takes me, wherever they are is where I want to be. And wherever we are, that is home.

CHAPTER 4

MOTHER'S DAY

*N*o matter what day of the year you are reading this, may all you mothers out there experience maternal bliss each and every day of your lives. For the ones of us who know better, though, may you be able to get through the day without words of regret pouring from your lips. This is my life goal, to date. I have lived my whole life to become a mother. It is my single greatest accomplishment and reward—not only because I count it a great honor to be the mother of two amazing children, but because I went through a grand total of twenty-seven tormenting hours of labor combined with these two little rascals.

Imagine the worst pregnant person you have ever known. Now multiply that by a thousand. That is me. I enjoy pregnancy about as much as I enjoy exercise. I loved the thought of that sweet baby being in my belly. I loved the baby showers and the nesting. But that cocktail of false expectations, nausea and hemorrhoids that I con-

sumed almost daily caused me to have the most miserable pregnancies you could ever imagine.

The day I found out I was pregnant with my son in
2002 was the most wonderful day of my life. I immediately felt attached to that little peanut and I could not
wait to feel all the feels that came right along with pregnancy and mommyhood. I knew in my heart of hearts
that not only would I be the best mother the world had
ever known, but I would be, hands-down, the cutest little
thing you had ever seen. I would look like Rachel on
Friends and I would be the envy of every pregnant and
non-pregnant woman out there. I would be able to stuff
my face full of Little Debbies at any given time of day
and not gain one ounce. I just had a feeling. And my gut
was always right. Except for that one time when it
wasn't.

My first week of pregnancy was sheer bliss. I was
glowing and had never felt better. Then it happened. I
had never seen it quite so up-close-and-personal before.
It walked in and stood guard over the door of my very
being for the duration of my pregnancy. It positioned itself at attention morning, noon and night and let no
good thing cross its threshold. Whenever goodness of any
kind tried to enter into my cells, it threw up its hands up
like that mean lady who used to work the crosswalk at
my daughter's school. We became frenemies, me and it, it
and me. It never left my side and it wrapped itself around

me like a warm blanket every time I moved or got still—breathed or blinked—woke up or slept.

Nausea.

I went from "pray for me" to "I need an exorcism" in about 2.2 seconds and I held steady for a solid four months, until I finally got to throw migraines into the mix. They were both really good to shake it up for me a bit. I never knew whose turn it would be. They always kept me guessing. And don't for one second think that I got relief by throwing up, because I never actually threw up. I just stayed in a constant state of "I'm about to" for the duration. During this time, carbs were the only thing that settled my stomach—crackers, toast, baked potatoes, repeat. So, not only did I not throw up, I also skipped right over Rachel from *Friends* and went straight to African bush elephant. I gained almost seventy pounds of honey buns, with rice and cheese dip rounding the corner for a close second. I hated everything and everybody but my baby and my shower gifts. All I wanted was to have that little guy on the outside of my body and to feel normal again. My son has always been a mama's boy, and I'm certain would've stayed in there as long as we would let him. If it was up to him, I would've been homeschooling him inside the womb. A few days past my due date, they decided to induce and I was all for it. I was ready. Had I known the pain that would make me want to claw somebody's eyeballs out, I might've chosen more wisely.

After eighteen hours of labor, I finally held that sweet boy in my arms.

He still takes my breath away.

He is tender and sensitive and deep and intelligent. He is sarcastic and witty and has a dimple that will melt your heart. He's an internal processor who would some-times rather have his teeth pulled than tell you his mys-teries. He hates to see people hurt and he loves babies and little children and if you need anything, he's your man. He is an old soul full of good style, great taste and a love for culture and the arts. And I dare somebody to ever break his heart.

Insert a few years in between, and it was the same song and dance with my daughter, except with her I gained *over* seventy pounds. Nothing new under the sun, except my craving bent more toward Fruity Pebbles than Star Crunch. Labor with her was nine hours start to fin-ish, and that same feeling of euphoric motherhood filled my being as I saw her little face for the first time. She looked just like her sonogram pictures and she had the prettiest little cheeks I had ever laid eyes on. She still does.

She is a writer and a creator and an artist and a nur-turer. She is loving and kind and would give you the last of whatever she has if she thought it would make you happy. She loves music and animals and makeup and drama. She is wise but doesn't know it, smart but doesn't feel it, beautiful but doesn't see it. And I dare somebody to ever break her heart.

My children are the best little things that have ever happened to me, and I can't quite remember what I did before they came along. They are my world—the honey to my buns, the star to my crunch, the cheese dip to my rice. And make no mistake. I am the best of the best. The G.O.A.T. Mom of the Year, baby! Except this is a lie.

See, sometimes I expect my kids to be sheer perfection, and even more than I expect them to be, I expect ME to be. I want to believe that I am all the things all of the time. Except that I'm not. My life as a mother feels like one epic failure after another. And I want to be the mom who, on Mother's Day, says, "I just want to do whatever my kids want on Mother's Day. I don't really want a gift. I just want to go where you want to go for lunch. No, really. I do. I'm a martyr. And I have an image to uphold that tells the world how selfless I am and how I don't need anything, not even recognition."

Yeah, right.

The truth is, most Mother's Days, I don't even want to go to church. I just want to sleep till noon like I did when I was in college, then take a nap two hours later. And I want my children to be sweet and clean the kitchen, and for my daughter to give me a massage and my son to smile at me with that little dimple, and ashamedly, I just want them to tell me how much they love me and that I'm doing it right, because most of the time I think I'm getting it wrong. That's what I really want. And maybe a gift card to Target. And maybe to watch HGTV all day in my pajamas. But that's it.

Now that I'm a single mom, Mother's Day has new meaning to me. Every day is an honor to be their mom, but a lot of times I feel like an epic failure. I hold my breath and pray I'm doing it right and that they will forget what just happened and only remember the good parts of me. Many days I feel like pulling the covers up over my head because I already anticipate my own downfall. While I still wrestle with my feelings of inadequacy, today as I reflect on all my mothering-done-wrong, I also see glimpses of mothering-done-right, and I feel proud—proud that these two people are mine and they have made it this far because look at how wonderful they are, and maybe, just maybe, I'm not a failure. Today I stand up and recognize that mothering is hard but I'm doing it with no instruction manual. It's not just another day of the year to me anymore. It's a mile marker. It's another lap around the track. Another year marking another day that my kids don't hate me and that I've kept them fed and breathing. Another day marking another year's worth of love that hopefully I've shown to them in ways that only I can. Another year full of mess-ups and mom fails and things I didn't mean to say, but here I am. Still their mom.

Most days I could self-deprecate and hate myself because of my lack as a parent. I could blame myself for every foolish thing they do or say, and I could count it all as defeat. I could tell myself I have done irreversible damage to my children. I apologized too much but not enough. I was too hard and too soft all at the same time. I screamed. I didn't say enough. I talked when I should've listened. Another ecclesiastical moment in the life of Heather Land.

Or instead, I could look back at another year and at that dirty kitchen and say, "Thank you, God, for another year to be a mom, to get it wrong and then get it right. Thank you for another year of mercy and grace and tough choices and hard places. Thank you for the failures that make me stronger—for these little pieces of heaven on earth who get their stubbornness and good looks from their mama. Thank you for loving me enough to help me correct my mistakes, adjust the damage and pardon the offense."

Mother's Day has become a moment in time to honor the position we've been given and the women in our lives who have shown us love-done-right, but do you know what else it should be?

The day that we decide to, once again, silence the lies that tell us we're doing it all wrong. To gauge life by the mile marker that says, "Well done, girl!! You got this! Messy house and all! It's okay that you've made mistakes and that you missed the thing and you hurt the feelings. Today is a new day."

Yes, it is.

Today is a new day.

Start over.

Forgive yourself.

Show grace.

Love well.

Tell fear and self-doubt that you ain't doin' it. Watch those Hallmark movies in your jammies all day knowing that just because you do, your daughter is not going to grow up and be lazy and that your son won't grow up and want to marry somebody the opposite of you. Take it easy on yourself. I promise to stop self-deprecating if you will. I promise to stand up and show my children what it looks like to be proud of yourself. Promise me you'll do the same. Because you are flawlessly flawed, and your kids wouldn't have it any other way.

Today and every day, HAPPY MOTHER'S DAY!

CHAPTER 5

RUNNER'S HIGH

I am good at a lot of things, okay? I'm not being arrogant. It's a fact.

I'm great at winning conversations.

I'm great at verbally cutting you off at the knees while you're not even looking.

I'm great at not remembering to check my kids' homework and refill their lunch accounts.

I'm great at sorting my traveling pill organizer.

And I'm great at being an idiot.

One thing I'm not so great at, though—EXERCISE. Not only am I about as coordinated as a three-legged dog trying to bury a bone in a marble floor, but my desire to work out is right up there with my desire to hit the enlightening stage during childbirth.

Nonexistent.

I have lots of wonderful friends in my life. Some share common interests, like shopping, sushi, drinking coffee, being sarcastic. Oddly enough, I do have a few friends who love to exercise. How in Lord's name we ever connected on a human level I'll never know, but we love each other just the same. One of my best friends, Karen, has taught an exercise class three days a week for as long as I can remember. And three days a week for as long as I can remember, she has asked me if I'm going to come. And for as long as I can remember, I have given her the same answer—I ain't doin' it. Last year she had the nerve to ask me to participate in a 5K run.

"What do you mean by 'participate'?" I asked. "Like, you want me to emcee it?"

Sure. I'll do that.

"OH! You want me to RUN it??"

Lol. Naw. I'm good. Thanks for asking, though.

I said, "You go right ahead, but the only 5K I'm interested in is one that my next husband puts on my ring finger."

The gall.

She makes fun of my struggle to live a life of exercise and I make fun of her social media gym posts, and we never miss a beat. Our love for each other "runs" deep. But at that time, I didn't love anybody enough to sacrifice the warmth of my electric blanket for a 5:00 A.M. gym check-in.

Even years ago, when I tried my hand at CrossFit, I chose the afternoon class. And CrossFit—what can I even say about this? It's like adult hazing. Truth be told, it should be illegal. I signed up for CrossFit after my daughter was born, in a desperate attempt to shed the baby weight. The trainers were friends of mine—a husband-and-wife team. Sometimes I still see them and their beautiful bodies on Instagram, and while I'm so happy they are doing well, I can't help but remember all of the mean things they did to me during the longest three months of my life—like strapping a giant rubber band to my waist and making me crawl on all fours until the elasticity shot me back up against the wall . . . where there was a ball waiting for me to throw it to heights unseen. Or like all those times they just watched me lie there and cry face-down on the mat but gave me no sympathy whatsoever. Not one single hug.

I'll never forget the first day I walked into that death camp. I was wearing my hot-pink Danskin shorts—$2.99 off the Walmart rack. How do I remember? Because I almost died that day.

"Today we are doing kettle bells and bear crawls." I later learned that these were exercise terms used in the stripping down of my dignity, but on this day, somehow what I heard was, "Blue Bell and bear claws."

"We have snack time at this CrossFit?" I asked. I knew I had come to the right place! I had found my people.

Umm . . . no. Kettle bells and bear crawls—instruments

and positions that we will use to tear down any pride you may have walked in with, and forever and always make you ashamed to run into any of the people in this room outside of this facility. That's what they should've said.

Upon semi-completion of these confidence-sucking acts, the next task would be even more daunting.

"Now we're going to run."

Run, you say?

I said, "Yeah, I don't really run, so I think I'm gonna sit this one out."

What? Oh. It's non-optional? I don't get a choice? Hmm . . .

What was that?

RUNNER'S HIGH? I'll get a RUNNER'S HIGH?

Oh! Well, then!! In that case, sign me up. Can I be first in line?

Give me a stinkin' break. Who gives a flip about some runner's high?

Look, judge me if you want. And in defense of what I'm about to say, let it be known that I have never partaken in any type of leafy drug, unless sugar comes from a leaf, which I don't think it does. Anyway, look. I lived in Colorado for four years, okay? If I've got a choice between getting high from eating a brownie or getting high from running, which do you think I'm gonna pick?

I'm just sayin' . . .

A few months of voluntary torture went by when one day, as I was getting on my Danskin shorts, I had an epiphany:

I've lost fourteen pounds in three months . . .

Pretty sure I could do that taking laxatives.

And so I quit. Just like that.

Now I'm not saying you SHOULD take laxatives. I'm just saying you can. Shedding the baby weight is a hard thing. I'm still working it off and my youngest is eleven. Do as you wish, but don't say you haven't been schooled on your options.

Fast-forward to January 2018. I will tell you more about this experience in another chapter, but let me go ahead and preface it right here . . .

Being in the public eye is no joke. I take pictures at meet-'n'-greets only to find these unapproved shots being posted on social media. Rather than blame you guys, however, I decided against my better judgment to join a gym. Now, it is hard for me to admit this, see—being as how I make fun of exercise people and all. But I needed a little extra push and thought this might be it. And for a solid, and I do mean SOLID, ten days I was fully committed . . . for ten whole days. I filled my little water bottle and set my alarm for 4:30 A.M. and I drove through snow and ice to get to the gym. And I walked so hard on that treadmill. And I jumped on those boxes and even when I missed the box, I got up and tried again. And I wore my shirt that my friend bought me to make fun of me that said, "I woke up like this. #sore." And I wore it with pride. And I stretched those five-pound weights up so high—so high I could almost touch the sky. And I did those wall balls and I lifted that single bar up above my head so many (six) times. And I did those push-ups standing up until my arms shook like a Polaroid picture, and right then—mid-push-up—I realized . . . what if somebody actually took a Polaroid picture.

Of me.

Like this.

In this gym.

In this position.

I would forever be shamed in front of my peer group and if that picture got out, I would most certainly forever be alone and would have to learn to crochet and teach a Bible study and love cats. My house would smell like mothballs, and I would have to take public transit to the grocery store until I was a candidate for Meals on Wheels. I would watch *Andy Griffith* reruns and get up at 5:00 A.M. because I went to bed at 7:00 P.M. the night before. The most exciting my life would ever be is winning a game of Skip-Bo with "the girls" and riding in the front of the bus to the Cracker Barrel with the seniors from my church.

And that's when I realized, ya know what . . . it's not worth all that.

So, I quit.

Again.

I mean, listen! I feel like the right kind of guy can overlook an extra ten pounds, but not all of them can overlook a forever picture of me throwing up in the trash can by the rowing machine. And one day I'm gonna be sending you a wedding invitation to prove it. I'll tell you one thing: I would rather be a little squishy around the middle than to be living my seventy-five-year-old life trying to beat my best score on *Jeopardy!*

Sometimes working out can actually be hazardous to your health and can alter the course of your future.

Be careful out there, kids. It's a *Wheel of Fortune* world, and I ain't doin' it.

CHAPTER 6

JORDACHE AND FRIED BOLOGNA

Have you ever dated a guy who referred to himself as "Daddy"?

Asking for a friend.

"Daddy brought home outdoor Christmas lights!"

First of all, those are not lights. Mama knows her Christmas lights. That is one single light. And that one light sits in the ground and shoots the dancing measles onto this dilapidated house you live in—this house with no garage doors to hide your broke-down four-wheelers and neon beer signs that you use to light your weekly game of beer pong with the boys.

And you are not my daddy. Because my daddy would never refer to himself in the third person as "Daddy." And my daddy has things like lawn mowers and cable-knit sweaters and hair.

I know, because I'm looking at my daddy right now.

See, a few years after my divorce, I found myself in a

predicament. I could no longer thrive in what had come to be my home—Colorado Springs. I needed to move to my "original home." Tennessee. The OG.

I needed to be around family and support to be able to better provide for my kids.

So off we went.

Home.

No, literally . . .

Home.

I moved in with my parents.

Kill me now. I wanted to die.

Only two words could describe how I felt at that time.

Epic. Failure.

Nothing could be worse than this. Or could it?

"Hey, guys. We're so glad to have y'all, but if you don't mind, could y'all not touch anything or walk or move or breathe? Only sleep and exit quietly, and don't forget to shut the door behind you or you'll let the cold air out and our bill will be four dollars more than normal and what would we do then? Also, don't even think about touching the thermostat, because we don't do change around here. And don't forget to reuse your towels three times before washing them. Oh, FYI, we only watch the news in this house. And we are deaf, so every morning at six o'clock we turn it up loud enough for the neighbors to hear it. Also, if you do not follow these rules we will passive-aggressively make you feel so uncomfortable that you'll wish you were dead, or that the option of being waterboarded seems like the gift you always wanted but never received.

"Everybody understand the rules?

"Okay, great! See y'all in the morning! We will be up bright and early stomping around in case you are tempted to sleep in."

God . . . where are you?

You hate me, don't you?

My parents are the best. I love them beyond words. They are the best old people you could ever want to be your parents. They mean well, and Glenda my mom, she can cook. But look, I'm an only child and they've been alone for a million years. They don't know how to go backwards. They don't remember what it was like having those things around called "other people." They don't know. And the only thing they know how to adjust is their glasses.

Bless their hearts.

And bless mine.

Dear God, what is happening to my life right now?

I kept waiting to die, but every morning I kept waking up.

In my parents' house.

And every morning I rolled over to find my third-grade portrait staring back at me—those bangs, and that green cowl-neck sweater and pearls, in front of that "We the People" backdrop.

At forty years old, this was not exactly what I wanted to be rolling over to every morning, and it sure wasn't WHERE I wanted to be rolling over.

Come and get me, boys. I'm ripe for the picking. Just sitting here. Waiting. Right here between my parents on a Friday night, watching a romantic comedy. Waiting for you to come ask my daddy if we can go to the Chow Wagon for a burger. I'm a real winner. You don't want to miss out on all this goodness.

What? Oh. You think you'll pass?

You mean, hanging out and watching my parents fall asleep during Bonanza *isn't what you had in mind?*

Whatever.

Your loss.

Luckily, my stay with the parentals only lasted a few months. I was finally able to get my own place—me and my littles. I had been single for over two years now, and I had been just fine. But after a while, boredom set in, and the desire to get back into the dating scene became a real thing. I wasn't sure how this was going to unfold, since I refused to participate in online dating, but I didn't see it as being a problem. Despite my recent relationship setback, I still felt hopeful that dating was going to be a success. And I knew I'd been out of the dating scene for a good fifteen years, but how hard could it be? Surely it's like riding a bike.

And hey, you know what I found? It really is!

It's like riding a bike with no seat and no brakes down a steep hill.

It's dreamy—like the nightmare kind.

I soon found as I entered back into the dating vortex that my moral gauge was a little low, and so were my instincts. On a scale of one to ten, my judgment was clearly at a negative one hundred. And I'm all about a good country boy, but my redneck-o-meter was going to have to recalibrate as well, since my only choices were somewhere between Cousin Jed and a toothless, front-porch, banjo-picking hillbilly straight off the set of the movie *Deliverance*. The "pickings" were slim. But at least I could tell who a lot of these guys were by the giant vinyl stickers that had either their names (like "CORNBREAD") or the names of their businesses plastered across the windows of their loud, raised and pimped-out monster trucks.

My standards were also going to need to drop dramatically in order for me to accommodate the caliber of bumpkins showing interest—right along with my moral code and minimum age limit.

Now, I don't judge, but when you're forty and you're dating twenty-seven-year-olds?? Come on, ladies!

I felt like this was a ridiculous notion and could not believe the nerve of MORE THAN ONE twenty-seven-year-old trying to get me to go out with him.

Are you sick? Absolutely no way am I going out with you!

You must be joking.

I may not know what I'm doing, but I definitely know what I'm not. Twenty-seven—no way!

I just couldn't rectify it in my knower. So, I decided to go older.

Twenty-eight.

Listen, ladies. This is not about age, okay? There is nothing wrong with dating younger men. Trust me, I know. If you find one that you connect with and who loves you, you'd best believe I will be front and center at your wedding.

Sometimes, though, life doesn't turn out like you think it will. Sometimes you just want somebody to take you to dinner. Sometimes you just want to Netflix and chill, and by "chill" I mean watch a movie and fall asleep right in the middle.

And sometimes, you hit that point. You know what I'm talking about . . .

We don't like to admit it, but it's as real as the bags under my eyes.

Desperation.

Sometimes we feel desperate.

And sometimes we feel so desperate that fried bologna starts to look like steak. I'm all about some fried bologna, but not when filet mignon is even a slight possibility. See, sometimes when you feel stuck and lost and like this is all you got, you settle for what's right in front of you, whatever it is. You settle for regular polish instead of gel—for Walmart instead of Target—for Evan Williams instead of Jack Daniel's.

This was my life.

Me and Evan Williams.

Me and my fried bologna.

I never even knew I liked fried bologna. And as it turns out, I don't (unless it's with cheese). I just couldn't afford the filet at the time. And instead of waiting until I could, I settled. I bought the Faded Glory handbag (to go with my Danskin shorts) because I couldn't afford Kate Spade. And just like my purse, it all fell apart. It just never did fit right. It hung on me like a weight around my neck. When people looked at me, they knew I was hitting my all-time low.

My friends were all dumbfounded at my clear display of temporary insanity as I, unashamedly, dove headfirst into some of the worst decision-making of my life to date.

I took that proverbial pencil on that achievement test and deliberately colored in all the wrong bubbles. I spat in the face of every bit of right-teaching and good advice

I'd ever been given. I wrapped up my self-respect, put it on Craigslist and sold it to the lowest bidder.

I traded in my Louis Vuitton for a Jordache.

I picked the boys who needed the most fixing and I accepted the challenge. In my past life, I've been what my counselor likes to refer to as "codependent," and I used to wear a sign on my forehead that said, "If you are a troubled narcissist with mommy issues, I'm available."

I couldn't stop. I just kept entertaining morons. One after another, after another.

Men (boys) who didn't want to go on real dates and treat me like a lady.

Who lived like victims.

Who wanted to control and abuse and drink themselves to sleep.

Who had no ambition, no morals, no ethics and no style.

Whose idea of a good time was making Jell-O shots and riding around looking for deer.

What about the one who called me Theresa for the first two hours I was in his company? My rationalization at the time was that he looked like Bradley Cooper, so I did what any woman in my situation would've done. I just went with it.

Or what about the guy who roller-skated? I'll never forget the first time I saw them—shiny and black, with what appeared to be brand-new toe stoppers. Upon the assumption that they belonged to his little girl, I soon stood corrected and in amazement at his simple statement.

"Those are mine."

Umm . . . okay. What? What do you mean? I don't understand. You skate? Like, for a living?

Do you have a limbo stick and a whistle lying around? Am I going to have to do the hokey pokey for my dinner? I can't even walk across the floor without my knees cracking. But hey, if you have any of those giant skating rink pickles, I'll take one of those.

Please. Kill me now . . .

What about the guy who, knowing I went to Bible college, tried to impress me by asking me about scripture?

"I've really been wanting to talk to you about something I read in the . . ." (*wait for it*) . . .

"twenty-third PALM."

No, you read it right. PALM. Not PSALM. PALM.

I said, "One more time in my good ear. I don't think I heard you right."

Surely to goodness he did not just say "palm." Is he a palm reader? Is he giving me directions to the skating rink? Turn right at the twenty-third palm? My mind would not let me embrace the possibility that this was what I was dealing with. *Say it ain't so.*

"I want to talk to you about something I read in the twenty-third PALM."

There it was again. What to do . . .

I said, "Look. No disrespect, but witches and war-locks know how to pronounce *Psalms*, okay? I don't mean to hurt your feelings or judge you right now . . . but I'm judging you right now."

Dear Lord.

What have I gotten myself into?

Somehow, I had convinced myself that this was as good as it gets. All the good men who love sushi and good hygiene are taken—at least that's what I thought. So, I decided if I was going to go out, I was going to go out with a bang. "Heather. Get out there and see what kind of bottom-feeder you can dig up. Find the guy with the worst habits. Make sure he's an addict and a hea-then and on probation with a 6:00 P.M. curfew for at least another year. Make sure he spells like a second grader, that 85 percent of his vocabulary is compiled of curse words and for the love, make sure he has socio-pathic tendencies. I would hate for you to get bored. Make sure he goes against everything you've ever known or believed. Don't listen to your gut. And also, find one who lies. You're a great little private investiga-tor, so that will keep you brushed up on your skills. Go. You can do it. He's out there. Look high and low. Mostly low. You'll find him."

Oh, I found him alright. Hiding right there in plain sight.

And life with him made me want to die—right there within those moldy paneled walls. Right there by his limbo stick and his whistle. *Just let me drown in this front-yard blow-up hot tub, God. I deserve it. For this life choice I have consciously made, I deserve only death. There's nothing left for me out there. I'm destined for a life of skating rink music and Donkey Kong. Bury me in a giant box of menthols right underneath the neon Budweiser sign.*

Now listen. Know this. Mama didn't WANT to be with someone who spelled "can't" like "caint" and "deal" like "dill." I didn't want to be with someone who always had another girl waiting behind door #3, but I felt trapped. Trapped by my own insecurity and desperation.

I wanted to do other things besides go muddin' and make deer jerky (however delicious it may have been) and be talked down to like I was worthless. I didn't want my poor choices and the men I was allowing into my world to teach my kids that it's okay to not take ownership of your life and be a victim and self-medicate to cover up the pain of a broken past. But I couldn't seem to break away. Because I was broken, too. I was about as unhappy as I'd ever been, but my loss of hope still would not allow me to walk away.

To my wonder, those friends and family members who were madder than a nest full of hornets at what I was doing were also the ones who extended their hands and helped pull me out of the hole I had dug for myself. A couple of them found the nearest exit, but the good ones stayed and helped me recover. They saw my destiny and potential and would not let me keep lying in that pigpen. I even made some beautiful new friends along that dark path—friends I would've never made had I not gone down that lonesome road. One, in particular, helped yank me out by the hair on my head. She understood my pain like no other, because she had lived it, too. We are an unlikely pair from different walks of life, but our experience has bonded us for the long haul. Some of my "friends" just could not hang in there for the duration. I guess the disappointment of my life choices was too much for them to take. One in particular, who I thought to be one of the best, decided it was time for us to say good-bye. She could no longer deal with who I had turned into. She walked away and closed the door behind her. Sometimes our poor decisions affect many more facets of our lives than we can ever imagine, and the repercussions can be great. Still, God was sweet to give me the ones I needed, and the ones who held up my arms, unfazed by my poor judgment. The ones who didn't make it about them, but committed to being there for me. The ones who showed me what true friendship really looks like. To say I'm eternally grateful to all those who never left my side is an understatement. Crawling my way out of the wound was a long, painful process. Taking ownership of my life and what I had gotten myself into was a difficult task, and being intentional with the work that lay ahead was not going to be an easy job. But staying in the mess I had made, I learned, was way harder. And dragging my kids along for the ride was even worse.

It was time to pull myself up by my bootstraps and start being who I knew I was destined to be.

I finally, with the help of Jesus, Nutella and counseling, woke up and got the courage to find the nearest exit and run like the wind. And I never looked back.

Listen, I'm not saying that I'm better than you, dude . . . but I'm better than you. Now, excuse me while I go find my self-worth. I think I left it on the other side of your beat-up front door that won't close all the way.

Boy, 'bye!

Mama is outta here!

She gone!

I hope you can find somebody else to take the mental beat-down and make cigarette runs for you. It was fun (miserable) while it lasted, but a life of class and over-the-state-line dinners is calling my name. Your 6:00 curfew just ain't cuttin' it for me anymore.

Sometimes it feels easier to stay put—easier than working on ourselves. But staying is the hardest kind of work. Staying in unhealthy situations just prolongs the joy and the destiny. Sometimes that good thing that's up ahead is worth the wait. And it's worth the work.

I don't know about you, but I'm doing the work and holding out for the filet. You can keep your bologna. I would rather sit at home alone on a Friday night and cut my toenails with a butter knife.

I ain't doin' it.

CHAPTER 7

SOCIAL MEDIA

"*B*ack in my day." How many times have we heard these words from those, our elders? But seriously, *back in my day*, there was no such thing as social media. There also were no such things as cell phones, to my knowledge, until 1994, when Candace Blakemore had one in her car . . . in a bag. We played with that thing for hours on end like five-year-olds on Christmas morning. Sadly, she was the only one with a cell phone, so the only calls we could make were to home phones or businesses.

Let the pranking commence.

Social media back in my day consisted of making a live appearance at the latest party or seeing how many times your picture popped up in the class yearbook. And can I just say, I killed it my senior year. If the yearbook was Facebook, then I was all over that newsfeed. The picture of me and my boyfriend-at-the-time served as an official Facebook "IN A RELATIONSHIP" status.

And all the photos of me and my girlfriends served as your official "GIRLS' NIGHT OUT/LOOK AT HOW CUTE I AM" updates. We ruled "social media" . . . back in my day.

Today, social media has taken on a different meaning. Currently, my newsfeed is eaten up with more garbage, lies and nonsense from people I've known for most of my life, but who still try to make me and their 1,000-plus Facebook friends think they're something they're not. We use social media to promote our latest business venture, to escape life, to stalk and spy and see the latest thing we can compare ourselves to. And we use it for attention. And I do mean WE. I am guilty of all these things. We like to tell ourselves that we just want to "share" our lives with those around us, and a lot of the time, this is a fact. But truth be told, many times we only want to share the good stuff. Which begs the question, why is a selfie of you flexing in the bathroom mirror "the good stuff"?

In a world that tells us we need to be more *this*, to look more *that*, we use our online platforms to protest that we are, indeed, all of those things and more. Even though, fact is, we are not. No one is. Even the ones who are . . . aren't. No one is all of the things. But I'll tell you what, your Insta-story says otherwise. Who even needs to make the cover of the *Sports Illustrated* Swimsuit Edition anymore? With all that photo-editing you just spent hours perfecting, and all those bikini shots you posted during your work hours, men will never have to make that magazine purchase at the convenience store again.

Thank you, toddler-mom, for posting continual catalogs of your perfect life, including your perfect child who potty-trained at nine months, eats with a fork and can recite all the state capitals. And thank you, CrossFit-checker-inners, who so diligently let us know that you got in your WOD this morning before my feet ever hit the floor. You are a picture of perfection. Except for one thing . . . you're not.

We are not.

But for some reason, our need to portray a life of accomplishment far outweighs our desire to illustrate truth and actuality. Funny thing is, ironically, we as humans don't crave relationships of perfection. We crave relationships of authenticity. We don't actually want to believe your life is faultless. We ache to see photos of dishes in your sink, of you in a swim skirt with your hair matted to your head. We would give anything to see your stretch marks and your disgusting house and hear the story of you losing your mind over your fifteen-year-old. Please, for the love of all things holy, give me something relatable. Give me a sign that I'm not alone. Show me that my world is not foreign, that we are of the same planet, that you are real. Touchable. And I'm not talking about touching your muscles. Speaking of, why are you always posting pictures of yourself? Let's begin by dissecting a few of these now acceptable means of social communication . . .

SELFIES

We live life not to make the world a better place, stand up for truth and justice or take up for the underdog. No, we live to post selfies. *Look at me. And look at me with my lips pursed like a duck. In my mind, this makes me look more attractive, more sensual, more desirable. Also, could you feed me a grub worm or a piece of bread while you're at it, because this little duck is starving . . . for attention, that is.*

Listen, just stop right there. I've posted a duck-face selfie before, too, okay? We've probably all done it—even some of you grandmas. But if we are doing it for any reason other than straight ridiculousness, we need to re-evaluate. Please let me see your smile. You are beautiful. Also, you're fifteen. I taught you in Sunday school. I do not want to see your sexy self as I'm scrolling through my newsfeed. I AM going to tell your mother.

Just be you.

One of my personal favorites is most definitely the gym selfie. Make no mistake about it, if I looked half as good as half the girls I see posting selfies in their workout gear, I would post, too. Maybe I'm just jealous, but enough is enough. We know you're forty-five and have the body of a teenager. Well done. Congratulations. Also, please stop telling me about it every single day. I do not need one more reason to self-deprecate. I can do that just fine on my own. I'm just glad to be forty-two and still be able to wear shorts, okay? It's all about perspective.

And what's with these bathroom selfies? Guys and girls alike posing in the mirror. For what purpose?

Here's my uneducated answer to the why—attention. *Look at me. See me. Validate me.*

Trust me. We see you—too much of you.

JOIN MY TEAM

Social media has now become the number-one way to try and harass our "friends" into joining our latest business ploys. Last week you were asking me to sell mascara. This week mascara is poisonous and you want me to switch to nontoxic, antibacterial cleaning supplies that not only REMOVE that poisonous mascara, but also take the paint off a car. Sounds legit.

Also, let's get one thing clear. Friends talk more than once every twenty years, and that's about how long it's been since I've heard from you. Now I'm supposed to believe that I magically popped into your head after all this time and something told you that I would be a perfect candidate to sell your makeup line. Right . . .

I tell you what, if you team up with a brand that

all-inclusively shrinks my fat while I sleep, actually puts the makeup on me while I'm cooking breakfast, helps me keep all my thoughts, as well as my calendar, in order and cleans my house while I'm out of town, cut me in. Until then, we're not "friends" and I would rather join a convent than join your team. What? What did you say? Oh, if I don't share your post with ten of my closest friends I'm going to die?

This leads me to my next topic . . .

CHAIN MAIL—TRUE FRIENDS

Share this picture of Jesus with ten of your closest friends in the next ten seconds or Jesus is going to come back on the tenth of next month and take everybody to heaven . . . except for you.

Share this virtual flower that represents every single person you've ever lost over the course of your life with four hundred people in the next hour, or your lost loved ones are going to come back and haunt you in your sleep.

Share this hug with fourteen people by tomorrow at noon or fourteen clowns are going to follow you everywhere you go for fourteen days.

Easy, killer.

Or what about—

Share this post with twenty people on your friends list or . . . you're not really my friend.

SERIOUSLY??

Never mind that we grew up together, that I held your hair back in college while you puked, was the maid of honor in your wedding, held your hand while you pushed out that giant baby of yours, wet-nursed your daughter and drove you to the courthouse to get a divorce.

Never mind all that. If I share this post—THAT'S how you'll know we're friends.

Makes total sense.

Do we really believe this nonsense? Please say no. Are we trying to be a good friend to the person who sent this post to us in the first place? Is that why we succumb? Or do we believe that if we don't share a post about how much we love our children, this means we don't actually love our children? I don't have the answer, but I know this: if I get one more stinkin' piece of chain mail in my in-box that says I'm going to hell if I don't share it, I'll hold the gate open for you.

OVER-POSTING/VAGUEBOOKING

These two titles combined could seem like a contradiction, but fact is, people love to vaguely over-post. It's a conundrum. There are people on my social media friends list who post on the continuum things like:

"Having a bad day. Don't ask." (*two hours later . . .*)

"This is actually turning out to be the worst day of

my life. I can't talk about it right now. Everybody just leave me alone."

Meaning, please ask and do the opposite of leave me alone. I feel certain there are a handful of people who actually are using these types of status updates as some sort of cry for help. For the rest, I'd say it's another deplorable means of attention-getting, to which I respond with . . . silence. I have never been a fan of manipulation. If this were the case, half the people in my life would still actually be in my life. You, sir, ma'am, are no respecter of persons. Also, please note that you are still on my friends list for entertainment purposes only. I digress.

Over-posting *without* vague obscurities is also a thing, in case you haven't noticed. No subtle nuances. No hints. Just straight TMI, too often. Please stop. Make me miss you. Make me want to know what's going on in your life. Make me want to know more about your trip to Paris, your new love interest, your child's progress. Leave something to the imagination. Your Instagram feed may as well be a see-through dress. There's nothing I don't see. Stop it.

Nobody wants to know what you ate for breakfast, lunch and dinner or what color your child's throw-up is. Having said that, let us take a look at yet another form of social media aggravation.

FOOD PICTURES

We all eat, okay? This is nothing new. But we act like partaking in a four-course meal is the equivalent of our wedding day. If the appetizer is the rehearsal dinner, then dessert is the reception. And I don't wanna see 234 pictures of your bacon-wrapped jalapeños any more than I wanna see 234 pictures of your extended family in regular attire sitting in church pews. Good grief! At least show me some smoked salmon with dill on crostini. And if your main dish is a casserole, ma'am, you may as well be wearing pants on your wedding day. If you wore slacks on your wedding day, much respect to you for not giving in to the social norm. However, excessive posts of said pants at every angle? Not necessary. Nor is it necessary for me to see the befores and afters of those twice-baked potatoes. Are you following me? Because I'm following you . . . for now, anyway. But any more pictures of your three-layer chocolate cake and we're through. At least show me your failed attempts as a peace offering. Redeem yourself. Show me how you polished off a bag of pumpkin-flavored Milky Ways by yourself in one sitting. Make me laugh. Let me see how you misspelled the word "birthday" on your son's cake or how your daughter's Hello Kitty cake looks like something straight from a horror film. If you can find the self-confidence to post THESE types of food pictures, you're my hero. Until then, stop insulting me with pictures of your turkey and dressing at Thanksgiving like you just found a cure for Alzheimer's.

JOINT FACEBOOK ACCOUNTS

Joint Facebook accounts always stump me. Nothing says "I trust you" more than a joint account. Why, though? What did she do to you? Who did you catch him cheating with? Is this the case? Are there other reasons? What would they be? Also, if infidelity was actually the case, is a joint Facebook account really going to solve this issue? Or is this your feeble attempt to "ward off" incoming possibilities? Maybe it's your way of saying, "Nope. Not on my watch. Because see, if you want to be friends with her, you're going to be friends with me!" Yes, I'm sure this will do the trick. Or maybe the reasons are of a more innocent nature. Take my parents, for example. They have a joint Facebook account. Why? I have no idea. Unless their online togetherness makes them feel more "one." Whatever. Either way, who am I actually talking to on here? Do you see the internal dilemma I'm having? And which one of you is playing Farmville while you're supposed to be working? Your only activity is purchasing goats and trading for hay. And I need no more confusion in my life. Please take a moment over dinner tonight to evaluate the real reasons behind your online tag-team duo. And one of you, please identify your true self and let me know . . .

Social media really does serve us in amazing ways. I have just written a tongue-in-cheek chapter on the everyday grievances of its like. But the truth is, I'm grateful for our forward-thinking peers who created a brilliant means for us to maintain a digital record of all our life's events. This platform has actually afforded me and my children a new way of life, for which I am eternally grateful. My hope is that, in a time and place where people insist we be better than anything we are right now, I can find it in myself to remain authentic. I will keep posting the good stuff, but I will work harder to post more of the bad. I will keep in mind that my pictures and my posts are a living record of the seasons in life. But having said that, people change, don't we? The way I lived my life ten years ago, even two years ago, is not the same way I live it now. I cannot go back and change my old ways. I can delete pictures, but they're already out there. They've been seen and heard and read. I can only go forward being conscious of the internal draw to offer the lie of a perfect life, and hopefully with the conscious choice to always live out the truth of who I am today.

Let's live consciously, remembering that the truth of who we are is enough. The good, the bad and the ugly. We are beautiful without duck lips. You don't have to convince me you are a good cook. Honestly, that casserole says otherwise. Thirty pictures of your trip with your kids to the zoo doesn't make you a thirty times better parent. But living authentically does. Giving the world the best you that you've got—that is post-worthy. And if that includes pictures of you on a field trip with your kindergartner (which it will), post it. Just know that our credibility doesn't come in the form of perfection. Perfection is counterfeit. Our credibility comes from the honest, the raw, the real. It comes from the heart. I commit to work harder at sharing from the place of purity and less from the place of persuasion. I commit to staying on the journey of finding the real me and giving the world all of that they can stand.

In the words of Oscar Wilde, "Be yourself; everyone else is already taken."

Wow. I almost made myself cry after that. I'm not sure why I'm feeling so introspective about a silly social media chapter. Actually, I think I do. There's a lot going on in my head. But I don't want to talk about it right now. So don't ask . . .

CHAPTER 8

OFFENDED PEOPLE

*H*ave you ever been offended? You've probably been offended by me. I get it. I mean, imagine how the boys will feel when they read about themselves in this book. Some of those ol' boys know I'm talking about them and they are about to be some "offended people." But make no mistake, my experiences with each of them has left me equally offended. I am offended at myself for dating them. I am offended that they called me by the wrong name and thought I would be okay with washing their clothes in an unleveled washing machine and coming over to pick up their children so they could sleep off a hangover. I'm offended.

It truly does amaze me how so many people can find the smallest things to be offended over and hang onto them for dear life. It does not matter one bit the topic of video I choose to create. Someone always spins it. Someone always takes my innocent video about how kindergarten graduation is excessive and makes it sound like I am somehow hating on their special-needs child who will never get to graduate high school. Never mind that said video was clearly in regards to me being invited to another child's kindergarten graduation, and never mind that it refers to over-the-top parents. Let's make it about us and get offended. Sadly, this is a real thing that really happened in real life. I am continually amazed at people's ability to make something so personal. The following are the types of responses I get to my videos.

> "While I normally love your videos, kindergarten will be the only thing my son gets to "graduate from" . . . for some of us, it's a big deal. It's an emotional event. To you it probably seems dumb to celebrate. But for a kid who will never make it that far, this is huge whether you acknowledge it or not."

Okay. Fair enough. But still, settle down.

> "Well that was just rude and mean that you would respond this way to someone who clearly wanted you to be a part of their child's special day. How heartless can you be, knowing it is serious to a child when they go from staying home with their parents to now being in a large group of people. You should be ashamed for saying this."

I am, ma'am. So ashamed.

> "I am offended by this post. How could you even make a
> video about this? Kindergarten graduation is a milestone
> to celebrate and help keep them going. It's a big change
> for them. If you ever do get invited to a kindergarten
> graduation, which you probably won't, you should feel
> special because the child will always remember you
> were there."

Remember I was there?! Are you serious right now? I homeschooled my own daughter in kindergarten. I did it all! I mothered the child, I wiped the child, I napped the child, I fed the child, I taught the child. And do you know what she remembers?

Nothing.

She remembers nothing.

She remembers that we lived in Colorado.

That's it.

Also, I was front and center taking pictures of my little man in his cap and gown at his kindergarten graduation. It's just jokes, ma'am.

Lighten up.

In one of my videos about stupid drivers, I made a comment about having to rededicate my life to Christ after encountering such ridiculousness on the road. This is the type of response I got:

"Your spiritual reference about rededicating your life to
Christ was just as horrible as the people that you were
complaining about. I find no humor here. I used to like
you."

My spiritual reference about Christ? That I have to re-
commit myself to Him after all of the curse words that
run through my head during my road rage? My comment that clearly shows that I am a Christ-follower yet
admits my falling short like the Bible says? That comment?

You people . . . I can't with some of y'all.

I made a video in reference to Olympic curling—
comparing it to sweeping my disgusting floors at home.
Now, hear me—I know these people are athletes, okay?
The greatest of the great. And I know this is a real sport
and I know it is not a fair comparison. Hence, the comedy in it. So really, there is no need to defend it. Yet, here
we are with another type of reply:

"I would much rather pick my teeth with barbed wire
than to listen to those petty announcers during the
ice skating segment. They are rude and disrespectful.
Those athletes have dedicated years of their lives to represent our amazing USA, just like the men and women
of curling did!"

Yes. We know. And we salute them. They have dedicated their lives and it is truly noble. Really. But I'm a comedienne. And I make jokes. And it's all going to be okay. Just breathe.

I made a video once about seeing a lady pushing her dog in a stroller while her child was connected to her on an arm-leash. Even then, people sent me comment after comment, vindicating their poor fourteen-year-old dog who could not bear to walk on the hot pavement, therefore needing to be strolled. I got comments asking how I could be so mean. Please tell me I'm being punked. Tell me this is not for realz. Yet I got this type of reply:

> "I can't believe you would say these things. My dog got sick and could barely walk and only had a few months to live. Going to the park was something she loved. She was pure joy, and this video is nothing but pure hate."

People, are we having a break from reality? Tell me you have something better to do than get offended about something that is not even aimed at you. Unless, of course, you are the one who strolls your dog while leashing your child . . .

Ladies, why, though? I'm glad you stroll your dogs and it brings them pure joy. I don't care. You've missed the point.

When I started making dumb Snapchat videos, they

were for the private viewing pleasure of my friends ONLY. Behind the scenes of my grown-up life, I was doing what every mature forty-year-old woman does. I was working a full-time job and making Snapchat videos and texting them to my friends. "I ain't doin' it" wasn't even a thing yet.

During this season of my life, I was having to fight my way through my own hurt and offense. Recently divorced, not to mention dealing with a life full of family issues and hurts from the outside world, I was having to learn what to let go of, what to address and how to set boundaries. Not only was I working a big-girl job, but I was having to do even harder work on myself. I kept food on my counselor's table for a solid year. I also feel like I brought endless entertainment to her life for the duration of our time together. She was a godsend and helped me gain perspective during that horrible, beautiful transitional period of my life. While learning to let go of hurts and wounds from people in my life, I was also having to learn to forgive myself for things I had done to others, and things I had allowed others to do to me. Clearly, there was some deep self-discovery going on. A lot of it, I embraced like a mean stepchild—with arms wide shut. Some of those wounds from the past I wasn't quite ready to open up yet.

Just stop with the "self-discovery" garbage, Counselor, okay? I'm here to find out why other people are dumb and mean and lame, and I'm here to be validated in my complete and utter disgust for them. I have only come here for you to listen to me whine and complain and tell me how right I am and how wrong they are. Save the life lessons for your kids. I'm not interested. My insurance is only paying for you to listen and shake your head. You're here strictly to be a "yes man" and to play on my team. If I wanted any lip, I would just give my children chore instructions.

I don't actually care to know why I chose to date the men I dated and just how I came to be codependent. I'm more interested in you agreeing with me on the severity of how distasteful they are. I just want you to be my girlfriend. I want you to stop the clock and turn off that weird music, grab a gallon of ice cream and two spoons and sit on the floor and cry with me. THAT is what I'm paying you for.

Thank God she didn't listen to that nonsense. Thanks to her I was able to get to the bottom of a lot of issues, and realize just how hurt I had actually been.

Some of my deep-rooted issues are for her ears only, and maybe for another book later on down the line. What I can tell you now, though, is that during this time of self-discovery I realized something. I was offended. Offended by people who had hurt me in my past. Offended by friends who had left me, women and men who had belittled me and family members who had left me with an adult life full of little-girl hurts.

I was so offended—so full of poison that I had drunk one sip at a time, year after year. I was no different from the people commenting on these dumb videos. And do you know what I realized once I got to the bottom of it all? I realized that the people who say hurtful things to me aren't mad at me. They're mad at life. Hurting people hurt people. They're offended. They're mad at the friend who deserted them and the men who belittled them and the family member who left them with an adult life full of little-girl or little-boy problems.

And then I realized the same about the people who had left me with huge gashes in my own heart. The people who hurt me weren't out to hurt me. They weren't out to get me or try to take me down because of something I did or said or didn't do or because I wasn't good enough. They were also mad—mad at all the things. Mad at all the people who hurt THEM. That family member who left me wounded was really just reacting to his own life wounds. That man-child who left me feeling worthless felt worthless himself. That friend who kicked me while I was down was wrestling her own demons and insecurities. The woman who crucified me to the cross all in the name of Jesus was fighting her own religious spirit. It wasn't about me at all. And at that very moment, I forgave.

I forgave them all. For all the things. For all of eternity.

Does that mean I never get hurt? No.

Does it mean I never think about it anymore or that it doesn't still sting from time to time? No.

Does that mean I let everybody walk all over me and that I don't set boundaries? Absolutely not.

But it means I don't harbor it anymore. I don't hang on to it. It means I understand why. It doesn't make it okay or any less real. It doesn't give people a free pass, but it does give them grace. And it gives me perspective.

It helps me know how to deal when I see hateful comments made by a woman, just to keep reading and find that she's battling a terminal illness while raising her three small children. Ahh . . . there it is. Her hurt. And today, she just needed a place to lay it. And so today, there's grace.

Now tomorrow, if she keeps on she's probably going to get a talking-to. But today, I let it go. Because hanging on is harder.

I forgive the ones who beat me down and tried to kill my spirit and who left me and didn't care and didn't love me well. I'm also not dumb enough to allow it to continue in my life. I'm not stupid.

But I forgive.

And I will keep forgiving. And when I get hurt again, I will reread what I've just written to remind myself that I have been forgiven much and the least I can do is extend the same. And I will remember that in extending grace to others, I am freeing myself. I am not called to live bound up in my own chains of unforgiveness, and neither are you.

So go ahead. Say that I hate animals and kindergartners and fourteen-year-old Maltipoos. Say that I hate Christmas and Easter and Jesus. He knows I love Him and He knows I'm trying to love you, too. You can lay that hurt right here. I won't pick it up.

Y'all can stay offended if you want, but I ain't doin' it.

CHAPTER 9

SUPERHERO

*I*t was the year 2014.

Wait. Scratch that.

It was September 14, 2013, to be exact. This is the day that parenthood as I knew it would come to a screeching halt. No more "Can you grab the kids from school?" No more "I'll be right back. I'm gonna run to Target for a few minutes (three hours)." Life as I knew it was about to change.

Enter Single Mom Life.

We lived in Colorado at the time and my children had been in what I considered to be quite possibly the worst school district ever, when their dad and I divorced. Let's stop right there for a minute. My kids may have been in the worst school district, but at least they were in school, I guess. I had tried homeschooling once before and am at it again, but I'm not sure which is worse—a bad school district, or my school district. I'm the first to tell you, I don't know what I'm doing, but I DO it with all my might. I digress . . .

My kids were six and ten. I had nowhere to go, no job and no money. I had no clue what I would do. My days of buying Free People shoes on a whim were over and I wasn't sure how I was going to navigate that. All I knew was that it was time for drastic change and that it would not be easy for any of us, but somewhere deep down underneath all my stretch marks and hurt feelings, I knew God was taking care of us and we would be okay.

On September 14, after enrolling my children into a new school back in our original stomping ground of Colorado Springs, I moved us into a friend's basement. We went to church with her, her husband and their four kids. Our boys were friends, so my son roomed with them, while my daughter and I took up the futon in her Mary Kay office. We had very little space and only a curtain for a door, but it quickly became the sweetest place I had encountered in fourteen years. I smiled every day at the peace I felt, and also because I knew that my friend Angela would always make sure my face matched my neck before I ever walked out the door. We lived there rent-free until we could get on our feet. Her house always smelled like cinnamon coffee and fall with occasional subtle hints of their ferret, Rosie, and her husband, Nate, who always prayed with our kids before school. They were the perfect dose of grace and love that we needed at that time, and their daily drops of ointment helped cover our open wounds so we could continue our painful journey.

I had no clue what was coming next, but I knew I needed to work. I also knew that, after being a worship leader (which consisted of making chord charts and mix tapes), a "real" job would probably be hard to find. Luckily, during this time, I had a group of friends that stuck with me like donut calories on my thighs, and one of them just happened to know of a family in our church who needed a receptionist at their family-owned business. Broken down and insecure, I went in for an interview. I feel like it started out on a good note—me talking a lot about all the things I could offer their company— until . . . oh Lord.

Here is comes.

The waterworks.

A full-blown come-apart right there in the middle of my interview.

"Here's the truth. My life is currently a living nightmare. I'm about to walk through a divorce after fourteen years of marriage. I'm alone in Colorado with only the help of a few good friends and my aunt and uncle, and I don't know how to drive in the snow. I cry every day and eat chocolate to soften the blow. I haven't had a real job in twenty years and will also have an absolute psychotic breakdown if you ask me a math question of any sort. Also, if one of my kids calls me from their new school throwing up or with a 99.1 degree fever, it's on me. So, there. I hope you find the right girl. Clearly, it's not me. Thank you so much for your time."

Then I heard the words that, to this day, make me question the judgment of the entire Cole family (and love them forever).

"You're hired."

I'm sorry, what?

I just told you—I'm a disaster waiting to happen. I'm a disaster that's already happened. I know nothing about nothing, including this job. The only correlation that I can make linking me to your screen-printing business is that I own a few graphic tees (I'm a little partial to Def Leppard). My life is a modern-day version of the Book of Ecclesiastes. Everything is meaningless. This is not going to end well. I will sit and I will cry every day and I will run off customers, and you will pay me money but I will come in late when school is delayed and I will leave early when they close for snow. Also, does either of your sons know how to check the air pressure on my tires before I leave? Because I'm not sure, but I think they're low.

"How soon can you start?"

They took a chance on me, and so did countless others. I will never forget all of my Colorado people who loved us best during that time—my family, one of my besties-for-the-restie, Heather, and her husband,

Daniel. They have moved me more times than a nurse moves a patient with bed sores, bought me countless pints of ice cream and even drove me to get a divorce. Friendship at its finest. My aunt, who gave me $200 a month to help me buy groceries for the first year after the divorce. My counselor turned dear friend, Yvette, along with her husband, Tommy, who did life with me day-in and day-out for two years. My friends Jared and Megan, who made sure my children and I had gifts at Christmas. And of course, the Coles, my family-away-from-family, who did all the things and loved all the ways and gave me a safe place to recover and heal for the next leg of the trek.

They helped me get sturdy for the days ahead (and I'm fairly certain they rigged our office March Madness bracket for me to win). They all assured me that just because I was stepping into new territory—that just because I was not the stay-at-home-mom I once was—my kids would live and not die, and that one day I would quit crying and we would all learn to adjust.

Adjust? How in the world would I ever be able to do that?

I have always been a very hands-on mom. My kids are my world and I have always prided myself on being present for all of the things—class parties, school plays and (the most dreaded day of the year) Field Day. But after these life-altering turns of events, and after becoming a working mother, I would soon find myself being lucky if I remembered to fill their lunch accounts and make it to a parent-teacher conference.

See, I was the mom the teachers could always rely on. You know, the one who came prancing in on registration day with check in hand and eighteen boxes of Kleenex and #2 pencils. The mom who said, "If you ever need anything, call me." So, how then, in one fell swoop, could I go from such heights of greatness to ground zero? I don't know, but I did.

I went from being the favorite to being the one who could never remember Picture Day and sent my kids to school looking like they just got home from a three-week camping trip. I was the one whose kid didn't get the Field Day shirt because I forgot to pay for it. The one whose daughter's backpack was filled with ants because I never checked it for possible moldy lunch remains. I was THAT MOM!! Over halfway through the school year, my son mentioned "Mr. So-And-So."

"Who?" I asked.

"My math teacher . . ."

Oh . . . right. That was it. That was the moment I knew.

My reign was over.

They ripped that crown right off my head and shoved it straight onto some mom who brought homemade nut-free snacks for the whole class with individual water bottles. I hated her. So what, she remembered Teacher Appreciation Day and her daughter carried a monogrammed lunch box! Who cares!

You know what, WHATEVER!

I hope y'all are very happy together. And hey, guess what? You can't take my crown, because I quit! Take your rhinestones AND this sash and shove it up your T-shirt cannon!

We're done here. I can't keep up anymore anyway. And P.S. I hate baking cupcakes and trying to Pinterest the latest and greatest creative ways to fill twenty-nine goody bags for EVERY STINKIN' HOLIDAY KNOWN TO MAN!!! I'm over it! No more valentines. No more Rice Krispy Treats (that never turn out right anyway!). Nope. From now on, I'm the mom who signs up to bring napkins.

And I may or may not even remember! We don't know. And if I don't, I'm sure you will all talk about me at the next class party. So, go ahead. Go tell all those tennis-skirt-wearing mothers with fake tans just how ratchet I am! Tell them my daughter came to school with two different shoes on. I don't care. Shame me.

But don't call me when you need somebody to ride that sweaty bus to the zoo. 'Cuz guess what? I AIN'T DOIN' IT!

To say that I needed a breather was an understatement.

Somehow, in His great mercy, the Lord gave me grace for the season, but I would have to find my center.

So that's what I did.

I found my center—a place where I could breathe and step away from work and all the questions and all the noise and all the homework and the Xbox and the arguing and all the life.

I found the center . . . of my closet.

It was my own personal panic room, my five-star hotel, and I checked in frequently. I snuck in there like a stealth ninja and I hid until I could once again form a complete sentence. The only thing missing was a Keurig and some Netflix. That closet wrapped me up like an electric blanket and shielded me from the outside world. That closet was my best friend. I went to it for everything. It knew my deepest, darkest thoughts and feelings but never told a soul. I lay on that carpeted floor and soaked its fibers with more tears than a Cleveland Browns fan.

I wanted to die in that closet.

Everybody leave me alone.

I'm happy here, just me and my knockoff Louis Vuitton.

What?

You need help with homework?

You can do it. I believe in you.

You need dinner?

Heat up a Hot Pocket. You know how to work the microwave.

Your tongue is stuck to the telephone pole?

Lesson learned.

Look, Mommy is busy—busy hiding.

Busy telling her clothes all the wrongs that have been done and all the ways to make them right.

Mommy is in the closet eating junk food that she snuck in while you weren't looking and solving everybody's problems but her own.

Mommy is in the closet being tired.

Mommy needs a minute.

Mommy needs to go into her closet and put her crying face into a thick sweater and scream so you won't hear, little one.

Mommy needs to deal with her feelings of being a failure for walking in late to your Veteran's Day program and missing your solo.

Mommy is trying to figure out how to work a big-girl job and still take care of you by herself.

Mommy is trying to deal with this new thing she doesn't know how to do called life.

But don't worry.

Right before she opens that door back into reality, she will see it.

She will find her cape hanging on the knob, right there where she left it. And she will put it on and she will keep on going—for you.

Because Mommy is a superhero.

All her tears and all her vulnerability and all her prayers have made her a force to be reckoned with.

In all her weakness she is still strong.

She may not be able to make it to Awards Day or be able to come eat lunch with you every week, but she is always there for you.

Aren't you, Mom? I'm talking to you—the one reading these words like you wrote them.

Yes, you sure are. You are a brave single mom, or single dad.

Parent, whose spouse works all the time.

Grandparent, who is raising your grandkids.

Moms and Dads who are raising children with special needs.

You are not a failure.

You are a superhero.

It's okay to go into your closet and cry and scream and eat chocolate and throw your shoes up against the wall (wait . . . what?). It's okay to melt down—to not be perfect. It's okay to order pizza four times a week and forget to pack your kids' lunch sometimes.

It's okay to be real.

And sometimes, it's okay to hide.

Just grab your cape before you come out. Know that God has given you everything you need to be a superhero another day.

You will live and not die.

You will quit crying, and you will learn to adjust.

You are not alone.

And one day you will be that warm blanket for someone. You will offer them the Mary Kay office with the curtain door, or the job or the Christmas gifts. You will tell someone it's okay that they missed Muffins with Mom.

One day you will come out of hiding for good.

Until then, know that you are still a superhero.

You're just on your lunch break.

CHAPTER 10

SMALL-TOWN LIFE

When I was a little girl, I was all over the board when it came to areas of interest. I was an only child who lived in the country with no one to play with except for the critters. My little West Tennessee town was about as big as my current Nashville neighborhood. In front of my house sat a cotton field that I traipsed around in year after year, and just past my backyard sat a pasture. It was full of cows that continually found their way through the fence and to my window in the middle of the night. More than once, my dad had to put on his boots and wrangle cattle so we could get some sleep. Amy Stewart and I sat on my daddy's archery foam on more than one occasion, eating SweeTarts and throwing them at the cows as they stared us down—boredom at its finest. Bud (my daddy) taught me how to drive in that old field—a green Chevy pickup—and I learned to shoot my first black-powder gun there when I was thirteen. My daddy was an avid hunter and he didn't have a son, so it all fell on me. For months, I had deer-hunting homework.

"After dinner I want you to go get you one of my Cabela's magazines. Find every picture of every deer in every position and circle where you should shoot him."

Shoot him, or shoot me? 'Cuz I would be fine either way.

My dad had a real knack for sucking the fun right out of any sport involving wild game. But he was wonderful—a great softball coach, the best man I've ever known, and he was the only man I had ever loved up to that point, so I took one for the team. Day after day I practiced. I shot that gun and I drew circles around deer shoulders. And when judgment day came, I was ready. I climbed a million feet up onto that tree that was about as stable as Charlie Sheen, and I waited. In silence (just like I did when I moved back into his house at forty years old). He had given me strict orders to only take short breaths and not to talk or do anything to disrupt the flow of life at that very point in time.

"I'm sorry you have to pee. We don't do that here. We are alive for two reasons and two reasons only today. We are here for deer meat and to prove to all of my buddies that my daughter can do anything their sons can do and she can do it better." Life goals.

Okay, then. Let's do this. I had been sitting in that tree for what felt like 505 hours when I saw him. He was majestic and beautiful and I hated to do it, but I knew that Mom made a mean deer chili and that my dad would be the talk of the break room for at least a month. So, I raised my gun, held my breath and pulled the trigger. That deer turned around and trotted off like he had nowhere to be, and my dad was furious. I kept trying to tell him that I nailed that shot, but he wasn't buying. We waited for another ten years, then slid down the tree and went on the hunt. And there he was, laid out on the ground about thirty-seven miles away, as sure as I'm breathing—nine points and about 175 pounds of I-Told-You-So. My daddy spun me around those woods like I was Cinderella. He even said "Hallelujah!" and "Praise the Lord." True story. He was beaming with pride, but all I could think was, "I will never live this down." We took that big guy back to camp and showed him off to all my dad's friends, who were nothing short of impressed. I sat in front of all my male peers utterly mortified, yet completely impressed and satisfied with my own abilities, as we talked taxidermy and tenderloin.

Dad ended up mounting my deer and hanging it on our Living Room Hall of Fame. He also made me pose for a picture in our local hometown newspaper. Up to this point in my life, I felt fairly secure in my general state of life, but at that very moment I considered running away. I was nicely surprised, however, that not only were all the boys accepting of me as a now tried-and-true deer hunter, but my cool factor actually went way up for the remainder of my eighth-grade year. This title of Female Deer Slayer stayed with me throughout my growing-up years, and made what was projected to be a most miserable experience well worth my time.

Not only did Bud turn me into the Muzzleloader Queen, but he also made me hold the annual title of Assistant to Angler of the Year. Every spring he took me out of school to be his date on an all-day fishing adventure. Due to his above-mentioned competitive nature, I finally got the guts to tell him, somewhere around my sophomore year, that I would rather sit in Spanish class and speak a language that I didn't even understand than have to be quiet for a whole day on the water. As much as I loved him and loved the lake, it was not my idea of a good time.

Luckily, with the help of some of my teenage boyfriends and guy pals, Bud's generally cheerful demeanor stayed intact year-round. Almost every boy I ever dated or was even friends with was some sort of avid hunter and/or fisherman, and they all seemed to come and go at just the right times. They all loved my daddy and my daddy loved them, and their presence in my life removed the burden of competition angler, game and waterfowl sportswoman from my shoulders on up into my adult years. They showed up at my house at 3:30 every Saturday morning not to see me—but to see Bud. They skinned deer and filleted fish and cleaned ducks more times than they ever took me to dinner, but I loved it. Because those ol' boys also opened my doors and said "Yes, sir" and "Yes, ma'am" and cleaned up real nice in their Duck Head khakis and Polo button-ups for a banquet or a wedding here and there, and I knew that there was no better influence on their country minds than my daddy. Bud finally moved away from animal sports and turned his attention to jumping out of airplanes. If I remember correctly, I took a brief dating hiatus, as no one was willing to jump with him, except for me.

I digress.

In my years at home, every boy I ever dated was closely watched through the plastic blinds from my great-grandmama Beadie's next-door window. If they ever stayed too late, she was on it like sugar on a sponge cake. I could never get anything past that woman. She told on me for everything from staying out too late to kissing my boyfriend good night in the driveway.

And why were you up at that hour of the night, exactly, Beadie Ann? That's what I wanna know.

I bet before she died, she could've told you the exact dates and duration of each and every relationship I ever had, because she watched those Chevy trucks like a hawk. She was particularly fond of the boys behind the wheel of the black extended cab and the green step-side, and so was I, but she would still rat me out faster than a cat lap-ping chain lightning. Lucky for one ol' boy, he just lived across the cotton field, so he never got in trouble. A few of the other ones kept me in hot water more times than you can say Beadie Ann Cole, but a few of them were worth it.

She may have given me boyfriend grief, but she was the cutest thing you ever saw—always shelling peas and gardening in her Sunday best. She could cook like a champ (which just happened to also be my great-granddaddy's name) and was known for entering her infamous recipes into the local Methodist church annual cookbook—the cookbooks that were passed down to me upon her final departure. Her little five-foot self was notorious for her curly purple hair, kitten heels that matched her polyester slacks and floral-printed tops, and my favorite, costume jewelry. She never left home without gaudy earrings and a broach, and I loved her for it. But if there's one thing I hope she passed down to me, it ain't her sense of style, nor her cooking. It's her nose for sniffing out shenanigans.

My friends all knew that if that white Caprice Classic was in her driveway and there was a dip in those blinds, they'd better walk into that house, head to the ground, because if there was even a thought in their heads about getting into trouble, she would telepathically know about it. And it wasn't just Great-grandmama that was watching my every move.

Almost the entirety of my dad's side of the family, the

Coles, lived on my country road—Salem Road. There were seven houses belonging to the patriarchs of my family, meaning I got away with nothing. Somehow, my aunt Elizabeth knew it was me every single time I left a mud pie on her doorstep as a child. In my high school days, any fast cars that drove down our road surely belonged to one of my friends, and any and all shenanigans that found their way onto Cole Lane was most certainly my fault.

Our house was about 1,100 square feet of brown brick, with paneled walls and floral wallpaper complete with hanging baskets, and if I never see hunter green and mauve for the rest of my life it will be too soon. My mom was a sweetie who worked and took cupcakes to my school and toted me around from playdate to playdate, while my dad worked and killed animals for food and fun. They were as great as great could be and made sure that I had any and everything that small-town life could offer.

My favorite person in all the world lived right next door to me until the day I moved away from home at eighteen—my granny. She was (and still is) my person and I loved growing up next door to her. I ran barefoot across her yard through every literal physical and emotional season of my life. I spent all my days telling her my secrets and listening to her stories. She made me cinnamon toast and wiped my tears after breakups and quoted me scripture and told me how I could do and be and make it through anything. She soothed my hurts and sang me songs and loved and hugged the life out of me. And she understood me.

She was a small-town girl, too. She worked at the electric company for a million years and was faithful to my granddaddy and raised two kids and did all the things small-town women do. She was not made of gold or fairy dust, but she was magic to me. She was what I wanted, and still want, to be. Strong and gentle. Sweet and bold. Calm and wild. Full of grace and wisdom and laughter. Full of love and patience.

Fearless. But fearless only because she had once wrestled fear. Gentle, but only because she had already tried her hand at coming on too strong. She paved the way and shared her life so that hopefully I could be saved from my own mistakes. She shared her anxieties from younger years and listened to my own heart full of concern so that I could, maybe just maybe, avoid times of suffering and dread. We iced cakes and tried on her earrings and looked through pictures more times than I can count. Her house gave me all the feels. It was my safety net, my panic room, my fuzzy robe and bucket of ice cream. It was Southern comfort, but not the cheap whiskey kind. And my granddaddy in his corduroy button-up, sitting in his recliner eating peanuts out of the can, he was assurance. Affirmation.

Their mere presence in that redbrick house next door was their oath, their word of honor, that I was loved and never alone. Even when I would find myself feeling alone, their continual deposits into my emotional reserves would keep me knowing I was loved and safe for the duration of my life. I am still living off the investment they have made into my heart. My granddaddy may be with Jesus, but his love for God and family, and his ability to laugh at himself in the most awkward of situations, lives on in me. And my granny may be quoting scripture to all her little friends at the Veterans' Home, and I may not get to see her every day, but her example of how to listen and love and laugh at the days to come helps make me tender but unbreakable—a force to be reckoned with.

They are iconic to me and my cousins, who for this only child are more like siblings. And they are legend in my small town. To everybody who knows them, they are revered and honored and spoken of with the highest regard. I love that small-town life has afforded me this great gift—the gift of community. And not just with my family.

My growing-up days were spent with the same people I started kindergarten with. We were all as close as the hair on the back of your neck. We did everything together. We participated in third-grade spelling bees, acted in school plays and sang in talent shows. We rode the strip, made homecoming floats, went to ball games, spent the night with each other, took vacations, went to church camps and dances and parties, and every Halloween, we rolled yards and drove through cemeteries so fast that the vanity plates on the front of our cars busted. We went mudding and ding-dong-ditching and even went to each other's family functions. Just about every boy I knew drove a pickup, wore baseball caps and listened to country music. And the air was always filled with the smell of soybeans and the sound of trains that wrapped themselves clear across Gibson County.

We all lived to do life together—it was the simple things. When we finally inched our way up to our junior and senior years of high school, we lived for one thing and one thing only—prom. Back in my day, when a boy wanted to ask you to prom it went like this:

"Hey. Will you go to prom with me?"

"Sure."

The end.

We got asked face to face. Eyeball to eyeball. What in the known world is going on nowadays? What is a PROM-POSAL? These kids are spending their life savings and giving away their dignity to outdo each other on who can come up with the most creative way to ask somebody to prom! Are we bored? What is happening right now? Save something for the marriage proposal, how 'bout it! Goodness gracious alive! I never in all my life.

Nevertheless, my friends and I loved prom season and we loved doing it all together. My girlfriends and I spent days looking for dresses, finding the right jewelry, getting our nails done, and then on prom day, you guessed it, fixing that hair. The higher the better. The '90s offered us so much goodness, but extra-firm-hold hair spray was probably the single greatest thing that decade contributed to mankind. Come 6:00 we looked like a million bucks and a million sequins, and we danced the night away and made memories that made their way into this book.

Small-town life added beauty to my life as much as Aqua Net added height to my bangs, and it had its advantages. My little town was like one big happy family, and being one big happy family meant only one thing—everybody knows your business. People in my hometown know what you're doing before you even know it. And when one person gets wind of it, so does everybody else. It's only a matter of seconds before your news spreads like shingles. And guess where it started spreading most of the time? The hub of small-town life—CHURCH. Oh, small-town church—I loved it. I still do. Growing up, if I wasn't throwing up or nursing a 104-degree fever, I was at church. And so were all the little ladies who loved to talk the talk. Some of them are gonna read this book, so I'd better quit while I'm ahead.

Small-town life also lends itself to some amazing

small-business opportunities. I will always remember pulling up to Doris's beauty shop to get my hair did. Doris was the mother of one of my friends, and her wild blond hair had me in awe as a child and the constant beauty shop chatter had me laughing under my breath till I moved away.

Some of my fondest memories growing up were of me and Sandy Ross walking down to Bobby Jones's grocery store on the corner of Middle Road and Gann to get a candy bar and the latest *Teen Beat* magazine. Hink, as we endearingly called him, was there every day of my childhood for as long as I can remember, and I feel certain our $1.00 maximum daily contribution kept him in business for the duration. We strapped on our jellies and made that quarter-mile trek and we thought we were big girls. This was a real treat for Sandy, because her family liked to buy old houses out in the sticks and she always had to get creative when it came to play activities. So, walking to Hink's instead of making necklaces out of tree vines and tracking 'coon poop was really special for her.

Our parents were also best friends, so every summer we practically lived at the lake. Sandy's family had a "lake house" that was built around an old school bus. The stove looked over into those green plastic seats, and I thought it was the weirdest and funniest thing I had ever seen. One year our parents decided to go cliff-diving and take us along for the ride. It was a three-hour boat ride, but we didn't care because we lived for the water. Our parents were not especially attentive that day, as they left us asleep in the boat with no sunscreen while they acted like sixteen-year-old hooligans. We ended up with second-degree burns and two weeks on bed rest. Parenting fail at its finest.

Our parents may have missed the mark on that day, but through the years they gave us a lot more than just sunburns. They gave us a friendship that would span a lifetime. Sandy and I have lived together, cried together, gone through pregnancy and divorce and the death of family together. I'm sure that big-city living also lends itself to close relationships, but I'm telling you—there's something about small-town living that keeps you tighter than a tummy tuck.

Small-town life is a beautiful thing, and even though I couldn't wait to leave, sometimes I can't wait to go back. I can't wait to be there on a Friday night and hear the sound of the band and the shakers and the cheerleaders rooting for the Bulldogs. I can't wait to run into my old friends at the gas station and run into my old workplace and say hey to all the people who keep that town hopping. I love going to church and all but having my cheeks pinched by the old ladies who have been gracing those pews since my childhood. I still think of riding the strip and going to the lake—of sleepovers and dances and my old friend J. T. McKinney, who we loved and did life with every day of our childhoods until we lost him in his thirties.

See, my life may have taken a different direction and I may not be witness to the beauty of small-town life anymore, but I will always look back on my days in West Tennessee with a smile. I will always remember my roots. I will always love pulling into town and going to see Sandy and pass by what used to be Bobby Jones's grocery store.

I think Kenny Chesney says it best—"Back where I come from, I'm an old Tennessean. And I'm proud as anyone. That's where I come from." I will always consider it an honor to come from a place where folks are grown right—with love for community and some good ol' Southern hospitality—because I would rather lose the title of Most Talented my senior year to Loretta Kidd than to ever forget where I came from. I ain't doin' it.

CHAPTER 11

CHURCH DO'S AND DON'TS

I grew up cutting my teeth on the church pews. When I was a baby, the pastor of the church would tote me around onstage for everybody to see my frilly dresses and chubby cheeks. My family helped keep those doors open and the staff paid with their tithe and offering for years on end.

Some of my earliest memories are of me lying in the pew when church went too long on a Sunday night. In between naps, I would draw on the tithe envelopes and eat Certs that my daddy always seemed to have in his coat pocket. My family took up the whole stinkin' row. Grandparents, uncle, aunt and great-grand on one end, my mom, dad, me and at least one or two of my little friends on the other—usually Sara Beth. Sara was one of my best friends growing up. She was a terrible child, and by terrible, I mean she would get so angry (for whatever reason) during church that she would claw her mother's pantyhose off. My dad took her out in the foyer many a Sunday to give her mom some relief and Sara's rear end a beat-down. Sara grew up, and, to my knowledge, never clawed any more pantyhose from the legs of another human being ever again. I saw her over Christmas while in the presence of her mother and I detected no anger issues whatsoever. Our friendship also proved to have no visible negative side effect on me, unless you count that time we got into a catfight and she scratched my face like her nails were nickels and my face was a lottery ticket. I digress . . .

Sometimes my sweet granddaddy would get up on Sunday nights and sing a hymn while Norma Lynn played the piano. This could quite possibly be where the seeds of my career as a worship leader were planted deep into my soul. I thought my granddaddy was wonderful. And ancient. My grandparents were the best things since sliced bread. My little granny, alive and well, is still the greatest lady I know. Both of them took home our church's esteemed awards of Father of the Year and Mother of the Year. Their presence in my life always made me feel safe and that this must be how Jesus loves me. If He was with me right now, surely, He would also let me crawl up in His lap and tell me how sweet and beautiful I am.

Growing up, my parents had their church friends over on Friday nights to play Rook while all of us kids played like it was our last night on earth. Matt Ingram, Sara Beth's brother, dragged me down the hall by my feet so many times that I had carpet burns running down both sides of my back on the regular. I guess it ran in the family. We had quite the crew when we were young. I can't remember how many times I played with Sandy Ross and April Deere after church on Sunday afternoons. We swung on tree limbs, rode four-wheelers and stomped through mud holes like there was no tomorrow. One time, we got stuck in a rowboat in the middle of a pond where April peed in a Tic Tac box. Besides the water, it was all she had. I can't remember how it all turned out, but I can promise you that I never see a box of Tic Tacs without remembering that day and wondering how she managed.

Until the time I entered high school, I went to my church's Wednesday night program for girls. I hated life and wished so badly I had been Baptist. They never did all that nonsense. The Baptist crowd did all the fun stuff—like played Ping-Pong and ate snacks and watched movies. They were all saved already, so there was no work to be done. Me? I was learning scripture and mottos and cramming coins into wrappers so I could win Little Miss Mile-of-Dimes. Of all the trophies and titles I could achieve, this is the one I esteemed to add to the heap—an award based on how many dimes I could turn in. I was an ambitious little gal.

Every year I competed in district art shows within my church's program, and every year my mother did 90 percent of the work while I brought it on home with the final 10. My contribution usually consisted of tracing letters of some poem my mom wrote, with some final stamp of authenticity that could only be deemed as my own personal work—my handprints. Every year I brought home a blue ribbon and every year I felt a sick sort of twisted victory, as me and Mom ripped the gold right out from under some poor little girl who made a pathetic excuse for a church out of Popsicle sticks. Where was this kid's mom when she needed her? Good grief! *Maybe you should've entered a different category, little girl. Like, interpretive dance. Was your church hit by a massive tornado that swept through the countryside as you were building? If so, then you are definitely deserving of that blue ribbon. You have represented your church well. If you don't get a badge on your sash for that one, then I'm not Little Miss Mile-of-Dimes.*

As I graduated from Wednesday night female scripture-memory classes, I was finally able to enter into what I considered adulthood—Youth Group. This had been my dream since I was little. I had finally arrived, and I was going to prove I deserved to be there. I was front and center, even early to the show. Week after week, I sang those songs and raised my hands and took notes in my Bible. And every week I rededicated my life to Jesus, since I was surely going to hell after the thoughts I'd had since the previous Wednesday night. I was every youth pastor's dream. I signed up for everything—every fine arts program, every youth trip and every opportunity to help my community. I was the good kid, which was not hard to believe after my youth pastor bore witness to Sara's repeated clawing of the pantyhose in our younger years. I was the good kid until . . .

I'll never forget it. I had on a 1991 off-the-shoulder, floral-print dress. My bangs sat up tall like a king on his throne and spilled over like the fountains at the MGM Grand. And there I sat—third row of my four-hundred-member church, smack-dab in the middle of Matt Pratt and Kristan Parks. Now, every Sunday, Sandy Ross and I got paid five cents for every note we took on that morning's sermon, but on this day we were not taking notes. We were passing them—between Kristan and Matt. And then it happened. Matt Pratt wadded up a note and chucked it right across my lap at Kristan, and caught the eye of my youth pastor, who happened to be preaching that morning. I was innocent and horrified, because what he did next shamed me for all eternity in front of every adult I ever knew, not to mention my peer group.

"Heather Cole, go sit with your parents."

Dear God in heaven!!

What just happened?

I hate you, Matt Pratt. From the bottom of the heart that you probably drew on that stupid piece of paper. You have let me take the fall for your pathetic aim and have left me mortified in front of my entire church family. I will never get asked to dinner or prom or a movie and most definitely not to this year's Valentine's Day Banquet. And because of this I will for sure never marry. I hope you two are very happy together. My reign as Youth Extraordinaire has officially come to an end, thanks to your immaturity and lack of athletic ability.

Broken out in huge welts all across my face and neck, I went out in the hall to be greeted by my dad. He was nothing short of horrified, as he would soon have to turn in his Dad of the Year badge, as well. Pretty sure I got the same treatment Sara Beth got during her pantyhose-clawing phase. To my utter shock and amazement, though, I was able to physically go back to church the next Sunday with only a flesh-wound-shot-to-the-pride. I did eventually marry a boy, although he was from another state, since from that day forward I had to sit between my parents in church. Pass the Certs. Also, shockingly enough, Matt Pratt and I are still friends to this day. He's lucky . . .

My life growing up in church has left me with a rich heritage and some great stories. So many wonderful and exciting people race across my mind when I flip back through my internal church Rolodex.

I'll always remember Joe Woodson, who did the Jericho March on the weekly whenever the Spirit hit. It looked more like *Soul Train*, which I was never allowed to watch. So, I always thoroughly enjoyed the live show.

I'll always remember Benita Todd singing on the stage, and how I always tried to stand right next to her and sing her note-for-note.

I'll always remember my uncle Wayne standing at the door, greeting every single person who walked in with the sweetest smile.

And I'll always remember Eileen Phelps. I loved Ms. Phelps. She is no longer with us and I mean no disrespect to her whatsoever, but she clipped her fingernails every cotton-pickin' Sunday until the day she left this earth. She was a sweet little soul, but her nail clipping, along with years of observation and life within the church walls, helped me create a running list of Church Do's and Don'ts that I will henceforth and forevermore adhere to. And please for the love, I hope you do the same. The first installment list reads as such:

1. No nail-clipping in church—as stated above. On second thought, hey. I tell you what. If you'll wait till communion when everybody's distracted, I'll hold your mirror for you and you can go ahead and bust out your electric razor, too. Let's just get it all

done in one fell swoop. You want me to run and grab an offering bucket and fill it with soap and water and shave your legs during the message? I'd hate for you to have to do the work when you get home this afternoon. We don't want to cut into your nap time.

Unreal.

Listen, if you feel the urge coming on, do us all a favor and use your teeth, okay? Bite those suckers to the quick. I don't care. But church is a clip-free zone.

2. Please silence your cell phones. We do not need to be hearing your ringer going off during the altar call. Besides the fact that it is going to take you one hundred years to dig that thing out of your purse, your choice of music is sure to be a Spirit-quencher. "Highway to Hell" may be appropriate for certain venues, like funerals, but the dedication of one's life to Christ is not it.

3. Don't save seats for your visitors in the front row. This is not where they want to sit. This is not a concert, okay? The Oak Ridge Boys are not about to come out and give you the performance of a lifetime. Jesus

is the performer at this show, but lucky for your visitors, He's everywhere. He performs in the front AND in the back. Seating your visitors in the front row is not going to give them a short distance to run to the altar. It's just going to give them a harder sprint to the back door.

4. Please do not bring a cold casserole to church potluck. The only thing more disgusting than this is you clipping your nails during the sermon. Nobody wants to eat cold noodles and wonder where they came from. Next time it's potluck day, do us all a favor and stay home till that Crock-Pot gets all the way hot. And while you're waiting, attending to your own person, private hygiene is much appreciated.

5. And finally, please, for the love, do not succumb to the pressure of dressing your entire family up like a Bob Ross painting for all major holidays. Ma'am, I'm going to go on and say it. Your husband looks absolutely miserable in that pink tie and mint-green button-up. Y'all look like a basket full of tie-dyed Easter eggs. I nearly picked your

son up and put him in my Easter basket.
And at Christmas last year I nearly licked
your daughter because she looked like a
dadgum candy cane! If you're gonna dress
up, at least make it fun for the rest of us.
Next Easter, come dressed like M&M's. I'll
take that over cold casserole any day.

You can do it, folks. I believe in you. Now, go forth and conquer.

And in the words of my home church secretary, Mrs. Rose—BE SWEET AND LOVE JESUS. You can follow the rules. Don't say you ain't doin' it!

Despite my sarcasm that runs deep on these pages, my faith truly has been the greatest thing that ever happened to me. And living life in those pews and with those people has shaped me. And while the church holds beautiful memories for me, it forever and always will be Jesus, not religion, that steers my ship. It will be my relationship with Him, not rules, that makes my life decisions and gets me back between the lines when I veer off onto the shoulder. It will be my desire to follow God and His Word that dictates my course of action in the end. And it will be His love for me that corrects and teaches and keeps me forever walking in His direction.

CHAPTER 12

SONG STORIES

I love music. I love it so much. I'm the person who, when I'm depressed, listens to depressing music. I want all the feels. Give me nostalgia lest I die. Oh, you're sad? Let's listen to some sad music to cheer you up! When I'm upset, leave me alone with Bonnie Raitt and a sleeve of Oreos. I'll see you tomorrow. When I am happy and living on the mountaintop of life, I'm like Tom Cruise in *Jerry McGuire*. I WILL find a song on that radio that fits my mood. Bet.

My love for music runs deep. My life goal was to blow my hearing and my vocal cords before the age of fifty—NOT to be a comedienne. I used to think I was going to be the next greatest singer/songwriter/worship leader of all time. I felt like worship leading was the way to go, since I'm not positive I can dance and only demonstrative hand motions are required in this line of work—and not even that for me, since I use mine to bang on the piano. I thought I would sing to the masses and sell five gazillion records each and every year of my life. People from around the world would sing my songs and everyone would come to know Jesus through my life-altering work as a musician. Yet, somewhere in the Lord's great design, He knew what best suited me, and now this career path he has laid out for me is one I couldn't have dreamed up on the starriest of nights. I am loving it.

Nevertheless, growing up, music was my thing, and hairbrushes in my house have been used as microphones way more than they've been used for their original intent. All during my growing-up years, when asked what I wanted to be when I grew up, my answer was always the same—"a singer." There was nothing else for me (or so I thought). Had I known I could make a living being sarcastic, I probably would've seen the gift and jumped on that train at an early age. Although, telling my daddy I want to grow up and be a comedienne probably would've gone over like a lead balloon. I also sucked at math, couldn't grasp the concept of a foreign language, spreadsheets or anything of the historic nature, didn't know how to cook, and the thought of working with children all day made me want to quit life. I didn't want to be an astronaut, a doctor or an attorney. And Lord knows I couldn't be a PE teacher. I can barely walk across the room without falling down. But I can sing a little. I can play the piano a little. And I can write a little.

Music it is. If my piano teacher from third through eleventh grade ever reads this she will most surely die of heart failure, as I had to be, positively, hands-down, the worst student she ever encountered. I can still barely read music. Sorry, Mrs. Ramsey. But she taught me to love it. Later.

She taught me to love the feels. She taught me to love the weight of the keys and the story behind the songs and the tears they evoked. She taught me to love the diversity of the times and she taught me that it was okay to mess up, and sometimes even suck. She taught me that music is an evolution and an art. It's an unfolding of life and time. It's a story.

Listen to the story. Play the story. Sing the story. Live the story.

And that's what I did.

In 2010, I got an opportunity to make a worship album. It's a long story, but the short is, a wonderful man in my church at the time funded the making of my first recording. I had no idea what I was doing. I had only written in the privacy of my own home and nobody needed to be hearing all that. My lyrics were lame and my attempt at rhyme and iambic pentameter was missing the mark. A dear friend of mine and one of the greatest lyricists, pianists and worship leaders I know, Jared Anderson, got on board to write with me and produce the album. It was a two-year process—probably because my writing was on a fourth-grade level and I had a lot of work to do. The first song I ever played for Jared was epic. I was about to rock his world. I played him my worship version of what sounded like "Mary Had a Little Lamb" and waited for his response . . .

"It's not blowing me away."

What?? How can he say that? I used the words "Jesus" and "holy" AT LEAST fifteen times. Whatever, Jared. Clearly, you're having a bad day.

But Jared didn't give up on me. And during that period of time I learned a few things. I learned that writing is a craft and it's a baby. It has to be fed and nurtured, and you have to be consistent in your discipline. I learned that constructive criticism is vital and not personal. I learned to listen. I learned that sometimes I write terrible songs, but sometimes I write great songs. Both are important in the process. I learned to be confident and relax and not let the song and the experience and the lack overwhelm me. I learned to be in the moment. I learned to be okay being me—whatever that is. Whatever I bring to the table is enough. Just bring me. God set this opportunity in my lap—in my life. Enjoy it. Be afraid, but don't quit. Be embarrassed, but don't give up. Sit on that piano bench after nine hours in the studio and let your tears drip down onto that dirty rug like coffee dripping down your throat because you feel stupid and insignificant and out of place. But stand back up and sing that line like you're Beyoncé.

The final product of that music-making process was an album that I'm certain doesn't even represent the person or musician I've evolved into, but it was meant for that time. For that place in history. It was beautifully produced, a fun experience with a talented friend, and a milestone in my life that I would never take back.

Fast-forward to 2017. When I moved back to Nashville after many years away, I reconnected with an old friend who is deep-rooted in the country music industry. He was like an old sweater that you wear on rainy days—comfortable. The time was right to go back into the studio and work on some music again, and he was the one for the job. But this time it would be of a different nature. My life had taken a different path. Broken relationships, divorce and single-mom life were new themes in my life. This music would be about the journey.

The making of this album was like intense therapy. I cried real tears in more than one writing session as I spit out the pain and the purpose in lyric form. I told the story to my cowriters and took them with me down the road I walked.

Each of the songs hit me in its own way the first time I listened, and quickly became a part of my story. Some are troubled and vexed. Others are upbeat and lighthearted. But they all represent a stop along the way. I wrote three of the ten songs on this album . . . the first of which would later become the title track. One particular song came way before I ever moved to Nashville.

It was after my ex-husband and I first separated. I was sharing a little condo with my children in Colorado Springs, and I'd set my piano up by my bedroom window where I could see the Front Range. Surely, these surroundings could yank some creativity out of this dry well. I prayed more prayers and cried more tears at that piano than I even knew possible. I felt God so near to me in a way I had never felt Him before. I even felt so close to Him during those dark days that I said to Him, "God, if this is how close I feel to you then just keep me in the valley. I'll stay forever." And that, my friends, is the dumbest thing you could ever pray in your life. Why would you ask God to keep you in the valley? Don't pray that. Because He hears all that. Shhhh . . . You don't really mean it. Keep that to yourself.

My heart was so heavy and full of emotions at that time, and I didn't know where to lay them. One day, as I was sitting at that piano, I decided to put aside what I knew to be politically correct in the world of Christian songwriting and just write from the heart. Jesus was in my heart but so was a lot of hurt, and I needed to somehow get it out on paper. I just started telling whoever would listen (which was nobody, because I was in the house alone) all of my hurt feelings about my crappy situation. I grabbed one of my daughter's school pencils and filled a page in some random little notebook full of six-year-old drawings and half-written-out recipes. *Why has it turned out this way, God? I did not ask for this and this is certainly not how I saw it going. This was not the dream that I have lived my life to find. Where did it get sideways, God?*

"Where did it get sideways," I felt, was not a very singable line, so I had a little more work to do. I reached down deep into the wound for more words to describe what I was feeling in that moment, and as I did, I started to feel something different from just the loss and the cut of the knife. Oddly enough, I felt some hope. Somewhere down in the pit of my stomach, underneath that throw-up feeling, I had peace, and I knew right in that moment that my life was not over. All was not lost. A sweet future lay ahead, and I was counting on it. So, after pouring what would prove to be only the surface of my hurt out onto that page and adding in some chords from my piano, a song was birthed. The meshing of lyrics and melody was effortless and seemed to just spill out of my broken soul like water from a boiling pot. I called my friend and neighbor, Yvette, to come and listen. "Why am I even writing music like this?" I asked her. "I write 'Christian' music, remember?" Her response . . . "To heal. For you—you're writing for you." Her answer was some sort of relief to me. And it was what I was counting on.

Counting On

I've lived my life to find the dream. I'm not sure
    where it all went wrong.
A love that's only made for me—that is what
    I'm counting on.
I know in time he'll come my way. Stand by my
    side so brave and strong.
Someone who's real, someone to stay.
That is what I'm counting on.
With me to the bitter end. Lover, fighter, faith-
    ful friend.
And everything he has not been.
That is what I'm counting on.
We live and learn, or so they say. Well, "let it
    be," Dear Lord, I pray.
And keep this loneliness at bay.
That is what I'm counting on.
With me to the bitter end. Lover, fighter, faith-
    ful friend.
And everything he has not been.
That is what I'm counting on.

It was nothing exciting. Nothing elaborate or poetic or life-changing for the music industry. But it was real. It was everything Mrs. Ramsey told me it should be. It was the unfolding of life and time. It was the story. It was tragedy and faith all rolled into one. I still didn't know what was up ahead. I didn't know what God had planned for me, but I knew it was a life full of good things. I was sure there would be more hurt and heartache, but I knew I would make it, because I knew who I was counting on.

When my kids and I left Colorado for Tennessee, the drive was so full of emotion. I was leaving a piece of my heart in that state, but, with high hopes, I was leaving some of the hurt behind with it. This was the place where it all changed forever, and even though my marriage had been tumultuous from Day One, this was where it all came to an end. This was where the ashes were scattered, and I was ready to quit reliving the experience.

I had put to rest the loss of the relationship, and now it was time to say good-bye to the hope that it could've survived. The fact was, it didn't, and keeping it on life support had exhausted me. It was time to move on and hope for a better tomorrow, and a better relationship. Little did I know what was in my future. Had I known, I might have stayed put, because dipping my toe in the hot tub of dating would prove to be just as exhausting, as you already know.

Anyway, I'm probably in the minority, but sometimes on long drives I like to turn up the radio. I like to get my head into the music and sing it out—whatever "it" is. But on that last drive home, every song seemed to fit my life and sing over me like it knew where I had been. Every line poured over my head like warm water and ran down my face like a river of tears. Scratch that. Every line poured down my head like a bucket full of alcohol and burned my eyes like a cut to the cornea.

And what did I do? I soaked it in. I let the words hurt me and heal me and I made sure I stayed in that moment, because later on, I wanted to remember where I had been, just as badly as I wanted to forget. I knew that one day I would need to look back and see how far I had come. I knew that one day I would need to help somebody else feel normal in their mess and, with the help of my friend Keith Sewell, we wrote "This Ole Radio."

Just these few lines capture the emotion of it all:

Packed up everything and left Colorado . . . If I
    had any courage left, Lord knows I brought
    it . . .
Right now, nothing seems longer than an Okla-
    homa mile . . . I got one hand on the steering
    wheel and one hand on the dial . . .
(chorus)
Oh, this ole radio plays another hurtin' song
It's just the way it goes when your heart's just
    holding on
Tonight there's a cold rain falling down
And your memory's hanging 'round

Oh, this ole radio just played another hurtin'
song

As you know, I didn't leave heartache back in Colorado.
The Tennessee dating scene lent itself to almost as much
dysfunction as I had known in my married life. Somehow, some way, I found myself in yet another "situation" that would inevitably leave me torn . . . again. If
you've ever experienced divorce, you know it is not an
easy thing to follow. A friend of mine once described it
as comparable to losing a limb. You have to learn to do
the simple tasks of everyday life all over again, in a new
way. You can learn it, but it will take time and practice.
It will not be easy, but it is achievable. Let's just say that
my process took a little longer than expected. Before I
knew it, I found myself right back in another mess—a
dating nightmare of epic proportion. I think I may have
mentioned it??

I finally got the gumption to claw my way out of the
hole I had dug for myself. It was an evolution. It was a
beautiful, difficult journey of self-respect and self-awareness
and I could not see what was up ahead, but I knew it was
going to be alright. I may not have been able to see that far,
but I finally knew good things were coming. And whatever
it was, it would be worth the wait. And it has been . . .
worth the wait.

There are many things in this life that I love—

handmade pottery, long talks with my girlfriends, flavored coffee. But if there was any doubt left in your mind, know that there are just as many things that I hate—being late, a messy house and driving in the rain. If one drop hits my windshield while I'm behind the wheel, I break out into a cold sweat, locate OnStar and map out a new route to wherever it is I'm going. Every worst-case scenario runs through my mind, including death, but mostly that I will hydroplane, cause an accident backing up traffic into last year and have to get out in the actual rain in front of this line of people who now hate my guts. Also, I will probably be wearing my pajama pants, but will probably NOT be wearing a bra.

Let's get real. You see, I actually CANNOT see. I'm getting old and so is my vision, and in the rain, it's hard to see what's up ahead. I can't see that far, so I panic. But you know what happens? I always adjust, and I always come out on the other side. Every. Single. Time. I white-knuckle it until I'm out of the woods. I pull myself up by my rain boots and push through the fear. And isn't this the parallel to life?

If you've ever gone through any kind of relationship fail, you know that sometimes it takes a while to crawl your way out of the wound. You don't usually leave a bad habit and immediately feel relieved. No. You crave that thing that is horrible for you and you fight it minute by minute until the urge is gone. You press through, knowing that what is best for you IS within arm's reach. You leave that drug or that food or that relationship that was detrimental to your well-being, knowing that there is something better down the road. The wait is hard, but the payoff is worth it.

Finally, there comes a time in life when you come out of failure and realize you're ready to dip your toe back in the water. When you feel confident again for the first time in a long time and you know that your contribution to a relationship and who you are is of great value.

When you're finally able to say: Listen, fellas. What is it exactly you're looking for in a girl?

Family dysfunction? ☑️

A history of broken relationships? ☑️

A woman with a shoe obsession and a chocolate addiction? ☑️

A woman with a smart mouth and an opinion about all subjects, including the ones that are above her pay grade? ☑️

But if you're also looking for a gal who's been through her fair share of junk but looks adorable in a headband, who is tenderhearted and loyal and will love you till the cows come home, I know somebody.

———

When I was on tour in Minnesota, I visited the Mall of America—literally the most gigantic mall in all of the United States of America—because I needed some new sandals for my trip. I walked into Nordstrom, and there they were—Christian Louboutin red-bottom shoes. I had never actually seen any in real life because I never allow myself to even look in their direction, but this time I gave in to temptation. I looked into their soles and they took my breath away. It was love at first sight. They taunted me to take three months' worth of grocery money and trade it in for a little bit of excess. Seeing as how I didn't have three months' worth of grocery money stocked up anyway, I felt like it was safe to slip a pair of them onto my feet just for kicks and giggles.

I knew that the five-inch stilettos would never be an actual reality for me—not only because I couldn't afford them, but because I would be flat on my face faster than you can figure out how to pronounce Louboutin (loo-bu-ton). So, I opted for the low-riders instead. This was the most gorgeous pair of heels I had ever laid my eyes on—the "Viva." Made in Italy. Square-toed, patent leather pumps with a 3.3-inch covered block heel. Slip-on style with a padded foot bed, and the only thing I really cared about—that signature red leather outsole. Endearingly named THE RED BOTTOM. The part that few people even see, but when they do, they are hypnotized—

bewitched by their beauty and captivated by their crimson charm. My heart raced and butterflies filled my stomach as I slipped the glamour onto my feet. *Dear Lord, I am Audrey Hepburn . . . Coco Chanel . . . Angelina Jolie. I am Grace Kelly. I don't know who I am, but I'm a movie star.* I knew I was wearing joggers and a graphic tee, but in that moment it didn't matter. I may as well have had on a Badgley Mischka gown walking the red carpet . . . in my red bottoms.

I felt amazing, and I wanted to die right there in Nordstrom. *Take me home, Lord.* I immediately texted a picture to my friend Heather, as to have a witness that these shoes had actually been on my feet. She promised that when I die she will prop my feet up in my casket and put me in a pair of Louboutins. And this would have to be enough for now, because there was no way on God's green earth that I could justify spending money that I didn't have on a pair of shoes that I was only purchasing for the bottom—albeit, the red bottom. Let it be known that I've never found a bottom more tempting in all my life, and had no idea that I was ever even attracted to such. I've always been more about the personality. I digress . . .

I loved this pair of shoes almost as much as I love my children. If these shoes were mine, I would monogram their pillow and sleep with them at night. The smell of the leather and the history of the French designer made me cherish the few moments I got to spend with them. And the feeling I felt when I put these shoes on my feet was euphoric. I was exhilarated. I was in love with this shoe, and I always would be. I walked out of that store like a whipped dog. *I will always love you, Christian. Never forget me. We belong together and one day we shall be forevermore. Until then . . .*

But have you ever met someone who tried on the shoes and spun around in the mirror and lived in the moment of infatuation, only to become disinterested after the excitement wore off? Do you know that person? The one you cared about but who could never be satisfied with just one pair of red bottoms? The one who couldn't even get them off their feet before they became disinterested? They treat people like they treat that shoe. I'm talking about that person who makes you feel insecure and unworthy because your soles are a little worn down. The one who, every time you walk into Nordstrom, is always looking at the other Louboutins—thirsty for the latest version.

See, these people aren't true shoe-lovers. They aren't in love with the beauty that is the heel. They don't appreciate what they're buying. They aren't in love with the aesthetics and the Italian leather. They don't cherish the real elegance and grace of the red bottom. They only like how it makes them feel. Keith Sewell wrote a song called

"In Love with a Feeling" that I think captures them perfectly.

> Your heart's like a tumbleweed in West Texas
>   wind
> Just blowin' from your heart to another dead
>   end
> One look at him, girl, and you hit the ceilin'
> You're not in love, you're just in love with a
>   feelin'
> Believe me I know, it's a game I was in
> He was playin' my heart like an old violin
> And one day you'll find, then you'll believe it
> You'll never know love, if you're in love with
>   a feel-in'

You've probably met people like this. Maybe you add value to them because you have a good job or a good reputation. Maybe you make them look good because you are beautiful or well-respected and you wear that Louis Vuitton cross-body bag like it's a Miss America sash. Maybe you help them with their children or bring money to the table. Whatever their reason for hanging onto you, the heart behind the purchase is bent. They don't cherish who you really are, and it's not because you're defective. They wouldn't know how to love you if you came with an instruction manual.

And you know it in your heart, because you can tell.

Do yourself a favor and show them to the flip-flop section. Better yet, tell them that they are shopping in the wrong store, because you, my friend, are a red bottom. You are exquisite. Your red soles may be a little worn down, but you have a lot of life left in you. You are valuable and worthy of an honest bidder. So drop them off at the nearest curb. Tell them you ain't doin' it, and go find you somebody who will treasure the Louboutins, because you're first class.

Of course, sometimes things just fit together like a hand in a glove. Sometimes you lock eyes and you just know, "That's the one." And sometimes, after the dust settles and the kids and the chickens and the dogs are running wild and you are stuck inside the four walls of that house all day, you get a vision for the finer things in life. Been there. Things that once found their way to your heart no longer penetrate your feels. You need more. That's why "Dream Kitchen," by Charlie Mars and Rick Brantley, is for you.

I met him on Sunday, he called me on Monday,
Took me out Saturday night
It wasn't three months later, a ring and a trailer,
You know when you know, it's right

He came home Friday, he was looking my way
And I looked a little uptight
Running everywhere, pulling out my hair
Cuz I know when something ain't right

———

I don't want no high heels
I want that dream kitchen
He blames it all on that magazine subscription
What does he know about *Southern Living*
Oh, he can't stand to see that look in my eyes
He gonna buy a dream kitchen

If I'm being honest, I personally loved this song because I thought the idea of a dream kitchen inside a trailer was epic. I thought, "Of all the things she could want, it's not a dream HOUSE. No. It's a dream KITCHEN. 'We can stay right here as long as we live, but I'm gonna need a gas hook-up and a new stainless, smudge-proof side-by-side. Please and thank you.' " No offense to trailer life. I'm all about it. But for me, square footage in actual living space would win out over square footage in my Frigid-aire. To each her own. Regardless, I fell in love with the melody and the fun of this song, and I knew that being a purebred country girl, I could own it.

Dream kitchen aside, even the best relationships tend to pose many questions. Like, why . . .

Why do you chew your food like it's your Death Row meal?

Why do you let your toenails get so long that they could cut open a can of green beans?

Why don't you take that ball game to the bedroom so I can watch some HGTV?

Bad breakups are also part of life, and part of the process of coming out on the other side sometimes involves a lot of questions, as well. This is my experience, at least. Some things just can't be understood. Some things aren't as clear as others. And when we are the ones doing all the hard work in the relationship, we are left wondering. And we have to be okay with never having the answers.

Have you ever come out of a relationship in which bad things happened to good people? You got done wrong, and that sweetie just kept hanging around to add torment and chaos to your life. You know their heart took that last train outta town months ago, but for some reason they like the comfort that your stability brings.

Do yourself a favor and walk. You can change them about as easily as you can change the course of the wind. No matter how much you care, you know deep in your being that it's just not enough. And it hurts like heck.

You just want to scream, "STOP! Just go. Leave me

alone. I'm too weak to say no. Just like me and my size 4 jeans, you and I are never going to work, because no matter how hard I try, I will never be able to whittle myself down and squeeze myself into a life with you. I keep trying, and you keep shoving me down, but I keep rising up like a muffin top. And just like my too-small jeans, you suffocate me, you leave me no room to breathe, and if I'm being honest with myself, life with you is about as comfortable as a button digging into my belly all day. I need somebody comfortable, who fits me easy. You no longer add beauty to my life. I want you to fit more than I want Girl Scout cookies, but you just don't."

If that's you, would you just lift your hand and keep it raised? Nobody looking around . . . I see that hand. Now, GO! Scream it at the top of your lungs and keep it moving. I promise, you will love yourself in the end. Because like my granny always says, you can't squeeze blood out of a turnip. You can't turn somebody into something they're not. As bad as you hate to do it, throw away your old jeans and go find yourself some you can breathe in. Jean shopping is no fun, but one day you'll come across that perfect pair. And when you do, the two of you will live happily ever after.

Until then, just wear joggers.

CHAPTER 13

DEATH BY HUMIDITY

*L*et's talk for a minute. Right now, this very moment, I'm sitting in a hotel room in Idaho. It's my first time here. If I'm being honest, I dreaded this trip with every fiber of my being. The travel time was ungodly, and the fact that I have a major event to haul tail to on the very day of my return didn't help, either. However, Idaho, you have beautifully surprised me. Your trees are lush and your streets are quintessential Hallmark movie–like, your lakes are slick as glass and you remind me of Colorado. I almost shed a tear as I wrote that. I think I love you, Idaho. I see us having a future together. You will be a place I sneak away to when I want no one to find me. A place where I come to write books, get in my feels, and hide from the world. Maybe I will one day elope to one of your quaint cities just so I can say, "I got married in Idaho." Who knows, but you're mine forever . . . as long as you can cool off. You are 105 degrees today, Idaho . . .

and I'm doing an outside gig. Who set THAT up?? For this reason and this reason only, you and I will be a seasonal affair. I'm not leaving you altogether, only during the times that you choose to be unmanageable. You did this to us, not me.

If we're talking about love affairs, let's hit the top of the list—COLORADO. Colorado will always and forever be the one that got away. I will love Colorado until I draw my last breath. I love its warmth, its cold, its sunshine, and even its snow. When I lived in Colorado, every day was a good hair day. There was zero humidity and it almost always felt great outside. I woke up looking like a rock star every single morning for four years. I didn't even have to try. If you ever saw a bad picture of me while I lived there it HAD to be the angle. However, for the first two years of my tenure there, the snow put me on mental lockdown. All I had to do was look out the window and see it falling. It could be minus 10 degrees outside, but I was sweating like a sinner on Sunday at the thought of having to take my kids to school. For that first solid year, my mind always took me back to the first and only time I ever tried to ski. My uncle Jay tried to guide me, but I was quite the rebellious student and was unknowingly on a pretty big learning curve. I was also on a really steep mountain, and so was the girl that I mowed down as I lost all control of my body and my skis. I saw it coming, but there was nothing I could do. I just closed my eyes, lay down and let gravity push me down that mountain until she and I were of one flesh. Luckily, no one was harmed during the filming of that accident . . . unless you consider my whole upper right thigh being bruised as "harmed."

After a year or so of climate acclimation, I finally came to love that powdery mix and all the things that came with it—the two-hour school delays, the fuzzy sweaters and hot coffee, the brand-new Hunter boots that it forced me to purchase. Suffice it to say, I loved all the things about Colorado. I can't feel my face when I'm with you, Colorado, but I love it.

Now, on to you, Tennessee. Of all the states I've dated, and if we are talking climate-specific, you are right down there with blow-up hot-tub guy. Now, I love you, but you have more weather changes than J-Lo has wardrobe changes. And your humidity . . . I just can't with you.

Seriously, can you die of humidity? Is that a thing? I'm going with a solid yes. If it is, then I've got one foot in the grave. Humidity in the South is enough to make me wanna quit life. Somewhere around the year 2000, I decided it was a good idea to get a pixie cut. "It'll be cute," they said. "You can pull it off," they said. "They" lied. This haircut was so bad, not only did I refuse to go outside of my home for the first few weeks, but I cried for six months straight until signs of life and hair growth became visible. The pixie cut is also not for girls with even an ounce of natural curl. Try as you might to look cute before you head out the door, all is lost the minute Southern humidity hits your noggin.

The minute I moved back to Tennessee, any bit of adorable I had went right out the window—right along with any cool breeze that ever thought about blowing my way. I forgot how stinkin' hot it is here, and I wish I could forget again. The Tennessee heat will make you forget that you hate your fat arms and will have you in a tank top quicker than you can say HVAC.

And what season is it, anyway? I mean, it snows ten months out of the year in Colorado Springs, but at least you know what you're getting—a foot of snow with no humidity and lots of sunshine. I go to bed in the 615 asking Jesus to keep us safe from whatever kind of tsunami, avalanche, ice storm, tornado or heat wave might be headed our way. Whoever knows. One day we could be wearing turtlenecks and thermal underwear. The next day we are in the bathtub with a mattress over our heads. Mother Nature either hates our guts or is experiencing some early-onset menopause. I'm done with her.

I guess there's one thing we can say for any season or incoming weather—it will inevitably change. Sometimes once a quarter, sometimes by the minute. For those of us who like a little spice in life, it's a welcomed break. For those of us who like predictability, this may pose a problem. I fluctuate. Sometimes I like a little seasonal spontaneity. Most of the time, though, I need a fifteen-day forecast so I can plan out my wardrobe. Even with that, it always seems to change.

Life is ever-changing too, is it not? As much as we would love to have a peek at the master blueprints, our Maker holds them under lock and key. I'm pretty sure He knows that if He ever let me have a look, I would be making some major changes. Hence, the suspense. Things have not exactly gone like I had planned. I like to compare the season of hurt I've experienced to the changing weather and seasons—a lot of humidity followed by some pretty harsh winters. I've had many days filled with unpredictability. So much change it made my head spin. And not just change, but unwelcome change. Sometimes it seems like right when I get comfortable and in the groove, somebody, somehow, has to go and shake things up. Drama rears its head and stirs the pot to boiling.

If I had it my way, I would skip all the sideshows and shenanigans and we would all walk around in our happy place 24/7. I would be skinny and be able to eat whatever I want. My jeans would always fit and my house would clean itself. We would live in a perpetual state of fall-slash-winter from here to eternity. Christmas lights and college football would stay on year-round. Pumpkin spice lattes would never go away and my hair would look fly on the daily. Summer wouldn't even be a thing. What is summer? There would be only enough humidity in the air to give my skin a youthful glow but not quite enough to make my hair resemble that of Don King.

See, I pride myself on having these brilliant (lame) ideas. Mapping it all out—no room for error. The fifteen-year forecast. I've got this. This is how I want it to go, God. Please and thank you. Let it look like this, Lord. Let me be this and do this and go here, and let others fall in line. Everyone would cooperate, not manipulate, and every day would be a good hair day. But the Lord has taught me as of late that there is only one good and perfect way and it's His. I make some mighty good plans (and some mighty bad ones), but He orders my steps.

The truth is, I don't really want to know which season is coming next, anyway. I don't know if I could handle it. I'm just grateful that the crappy ones don't last forever. Aren't you? Good grief!

I'm grateful that He gives grace for the tough seasons. He knows what I can handle. He knows that I would rather be in a cardigan but for some reason, that tank top seems to be what I need for the day.

And while I'm in the tough seasons, those rough waters, I'm glad to know who calms my seas. I know who tells the winds and waves to obey. I've watched Him do it in my life time and time again. See, I don't need to be able to look too far ahead. I just need to hold the hand of the One who knows what's coming. He's got me. He makes better decisions than I do. He knows what I need when I need it. And He knows what you need, too.

He sees what we cannot see. We only know part of the story, but one day we will be able to ask Him all the "whys" we can think of. Until then, will we choose to rest and be content following the day-to-day path He has set in front of us, or will we try to insist on the minute-by-minute forecast? Sometimes the choice to rest content may come easy. Sometimes it may be a moment-by-moment YES. However we choose to get there, I promise to try to embrace the season if you will . . . humidity and all.

CHAPTER 14

MAGIC EIGHT BALL

*T*aking special care of those around me, especially my children, is something that has always come naturally for me. Despite the nature of my sarcastic platform and my seamless ability to cut you to the bone with my words, I have this innate desire to please and to nurture. I am the mom who wanted to wrap my kids in bubble wrap and Styrofoam to protect them from the outside elements. I was the worst-case-scenario mom—Helmet Mom.

"Hey you! Child! Where do think you're going? I don't give a flying flip if you're just going to the mailbox. Put on your helmet!" And God forbid they try to jump on the trampoline without adult supervision. I mean, what would happen if they got thrown twenty feet up in the air and flipped backwards onto the chain-link fence? I'm sure I would've been able to get up out of my lawn chair in time to catch them and prevent them from a life of brain damage.

Being a hands-on mom has proven to be more exhausting than conversations with a six-year-old, but more rewarding than anything else I could ever hope to achieve. My kids are my world, which is precisely why I need to take care of myself every now and then.

Taking care of yourself looks different for everybody. For some, it's having a healthy diet and working out. Instead, I like to do other things that evoke self-care and preservation—like get facials. And online shop. And get my nails done. And most of all, get massages.

This is not something I do often—maybe once a year. But for my birthday this year, Tosha—my mostly companion, my friend of over twenty-five years who has now turned into my assistant—got me a massage. I think her exact words were, "I wanted to get you something special because you work so hard . . . at that gym you never go to." Whatever. Give me backhanded compliments all you want, but hand over that gift card.

If you've ever gotten a massage, you know that a few things run through your mind upon arrival. If you're a mom, I can almost guarantee I know what they are.

THIS IS GOING TO BE THE GREATEST DAY OF MY LIFE. And . . .

I'M ABOUT TO GET THE NAP OF A LIFETIME.

At least one solid hour of silence—only the sound of squirting lotion, tropical ocean waves and you, snoring. Occasionally, you will have to tolerate the sound of your massage therapist's voice as she tells you to turn over. We'll let it slide. Just lay your hands on me in the most non-intimate of ways, and make me feel like a rock star for the next hour. I don't care if you like me, how you're feeling today, nothing. I'm not interested in your small talk or your welcome speech. Turn around, let me take off my clothes and jump on this table, and let your fingers do the walking. We good? Good.

This is how I feel. Unapologetically. My skin is in desperate need of physical touch of an innocent nature and I'm willing to pay good money to get it. Now get to work.

The day I cashed in my gift card, my mind was full of all the thoughts of rainbows and unicorns and naps and warm blankets and hot rocks. When I got there, I had a coffee and waited patiently for my therapist to come and get me. I had never been to this place, so I had no idea who I was getting, but I was sure as the day was long that she was gonna change my life forever. And she did . . . forever.

She introduced herself, took me into the room and gave me general instructions right before she stepped out for me to get vulnerable. I slid down into those cozy sheets and stuck my face down in that hole that pulls your mouth apart. I felt like a tool, but I didn't care. I was tempted to yell, "I'm ready!!" because time was a-wasting, but I decided to show some restraint and sophistication, and so I waited.

Finally, in she walked. *Here we go.* I smiled down at the floor as I envisioned what was about to go down. Soft hands on my strained back pressing down on all the right muscles at just the right time. *Show me what you got, lady. I'm a great tipper.* Right at that very moment, the course of my day and my entire comedy act changed.

"I'm just going to listen to your back and let it tell me what to do to the rest of your body."

I know she did not just say that to me.

Umm . . . I'm sorry. What?? You're going to what? Okay. Sure. That sounds totally normal. You do that. I don't know how talkative it's gonna be this early in the morning, but you can sure give it a go. If you'd like to ask my lips, I bet they could tell you, but that would probably be too easy, I guess.

She pressed down for what felt like three years, then said, "I think it's telling me to start at your feet."

Good grief. This is amazing! I had no idea my back could talk. All these years I've felt so alone, and now here I find out I've had a companion this whole time and didn't even know it. I ask Jesus questions all the time, but it usually takes Him way longer to answer. I tell you what: if ever I feel lonely or in doubt, I know where I'm going—straight to the back.

And seriously? My feet? You have GOT to be kidding me right now, lady!!! That's just weird!! But whatever. Start where you want. Just let me sleep.

No luck.

"You didn't have very much for breakfast this morning."

What in the Sam Hill is going on in my life right now?

I had no idea how to respond.

"Yeah, I can tell from rubbing your feet that you didn't eat very much this morning."

Right. Except that I did—more than usual, actually. I ate two eggs, a piece of toast and some almond butter. I also snagged a couple of M&M's on the way out the door. So, WRONG!

I didn't even know what to say, so I think I just said something like, "Hmm . . ."

She proceeded as I tried to relax my mind once more to enjoy what I had still hoped to be my day of solace. It only took me about two solid minutes of quiet to begin drifting off into mental nirvana. I was almost there. I was at sleep's door, hand on the knob, when she said, "Athlete or dancer?"

My Lord and my God!! Is this seriously happening right now? Did you just ask me yet another question? So close, but so far away . . . And why are you asking me? I thought my back had all the answers.

I regained consciousness and tried to think of my best response. Clearly, this woman had no idea who she was dealing with—bar-none THE most unathletic person to ever grace her doors. How did she not know?? Those weren't muscles she was rubbing!! I finally thought it through and said, "Well . . . I guess if I had to pick, I'd choose dancer. I've always really wanted to do that."

She said, "NO!! WERE YOU an athlete or a dancer?"

Back to the drawing board. Hmm . . . Well, I for sure was never a dancer. But was I an athlete? I mean, I made the B-team my seventh-grade year of basketball, but that was only because "everybody got a trophy." I totally sucked and I knew it. I actually remember hoping I would never get put in the game. I just wanted to play because my best friend, Amy, did. That was it. Also, those high-tops were killer and I wanted a pair. At the time, both valid reasons. I didn't feel, however, that my time on the bench was nearly as strenuous as my time in marching band.

There was my answer.

"Well, I played French horn in the seventh-grade marching band. Does that count?"

No answer. Thank God! Maybe my under-the-radar sarcasm left her with just enough bitter in her mouth to keep that thing shut.

Working her way up my body, she got to my glutes. I promise you this, that lady dug her forearm so deep into my left butt cheek that I felt like I was on a wrestling mat. I thought to myself, "If she does not let up in three seconds I'm tapping out!" She was taking my breath away. All of the sudden she said, "Oh man! Somebody's doing some squats!"

I jerked my head up out of that hole and said, "WHO? I thought we were in here alone!!" Because mark my words, it was not I who had been squatting. Now, if she had said, "Somebody's been doing some sitting," then I would've understood. But squats? Negative.

Why are we even together, lady? Clearly, you don't even know me anymore. I feel a breakup coming on.

We were at the halfway mark and all I could think was "Is it over yet? Am I being punished, God?" And then I heard Him answer. His voice sounded like a whoopie cushion as she so very aggressively squirted giant drops of lotion from an almost-empty bottle straight onto my back.

"Yes. You are being punished."

I hear you, Lord.

And for whatever I have done to deserve this punishment, I am truly sorry.

Look, I'm no genius, but I'm fairly certain this was covered in Massage Therapy 101. *What is the matter with you, lady? Don't you know you're supposed to squirt that mess into your hands first? Heat it up a little before you go dropping those liquid ice cubes on my back. Good Lord!*

Not only did she squirt it directly onto my back, but she didn't even rub it in. I looked up a couple of times to see where the wind from the oscillating fan was coming from. *Wha . . . are you . . . are you blowing on my back? What are you doing? Are you even touching me? You go from digging down to my butt bone to rubbing my back with a feather duster? What is happening? What is this hoo-doo you've got going on back there? Am I in a work-study?*

Wait . . . Is that a paintbrush you're holding? Are you Bob Ross?! That tight perm and those brushstrokes tell me "maybe." On second thought, I'm going with a solid yes on that. Can't wait to see all the "happy little trees" you've so gracefully painted upon my back. I can just about guarantee you they are the only things happy on my body right now!

Just when I thought it couldn't get any worse, she got her little doctor's chair and wheeled around to my head. Afraid to open my eyes, I finally took a peek, only to see her legs right underneath my face. She stuck her hands in my hair for what I was hoping to be a scalp massage. *Surely she can't mess this up. Oh, wait. Yes, she can.*

This was no scalp massage. *What is going on up there? I mean, besides the fact that you're coughing all over my head like you just stepped out and smoked a pack of Pall Malls. Are you braiding my hair? Oh my Lord, are we in the Bahamas?* This lady somehow managed to have her fingers intertwined in each and every follicle of my hair without actually even touching my scalp the first time. I wish I would've taken a picture when I got up. I looked like Jack Nicholson when I sat up off that table.

After my head was used for what was sure to be a beauty school demonstration, I had the most beautiful thought.

I think it's almost over.

This thought frustrated me more than having to fill out my divorce papers. This was not how it should be. I should be walking away satisfied and rejuvenated. Instead, I was going to have to go park at Kroger to squeeze in a ten-minute recovery nap before I headed back home. Lord knows I wouldn't be getting one there. She was working her way down to my shoulders, so surely, any day now . . .

Just as her hands dug their way into my shoulders, she did it again.

"Basketball or volleyball?"

LISTEN HERE, LADY!! I can't take it another second! You couldn't be more wrong if you tried.

Stop it! Quit guessing! You have missed every question on the test today. Lay down your pencil and walk away. Just quit. Sometimes it's okay to be a quitter. Today is that day.

I had about as much nice left in me as that lotion bottle she used on my back.

Look. I really appreciate you penciling me in today . . . PROPHETESS.

Clearly the batteries on your magic eight ball are running a little low today. I'm gonna need you to work a little bit more on my muscles, and a little bit less on my nerves.

By this time it was too late. It was over. I felt menopausal, as I went through just about every emotion available in a thirty-second time span.

Utter disappointment.

Uncontrollable sadness.

Severe fatigue.

Intense anger.

Bottomless rage.

I couldn't believe it was over. I can only compare my emotional state to the same way I felt when my daughter slept through the night for the first time.

If I remember correctly, I ugly cried. Both times.

I hugged that woman tighter than the fit on my blue jeans. *Thank you! Thank you for releasing me. I don't know why I'm hugging you. I feel like I'm experiencing a touch of Stockholm syndrome. You know, when the hostage feels endeared to their captor? Thank you for that brutal mistreatment. I must've deserved it. Also, I'll make another appointment and come back for more of your terrorism soon. In just a few short weeks we will be together again.*

Just kidding.

That last paragraph is nothing but straight lies. Because I threw my clothes on faster than you can say Bob Ross. And I'm pretty sure she knew from the thank-you I uttered between gritted teeth and my undeniable stink-eye that I would, in fact, never be checking into this torture chamber ever again. *Peace out, lady. I hope your next victim makes it out alive and I hope you come to the firm realization that this is not your calling. Either way, sure as I'm still breathing, I will never be bound to your table again for as long as we both shall live. I ain't doin' it.*

See, I walked into that massage room with an expectation. A false one. I had built up this day in my mind to the point that when this lady did not deliver, I was as devastated as I was the day *Fixer Upper* announced their last season. Nothing could've prepared me or consoled me.

I was convinced it should be this way and no other way, and while this was definitely an unconventional approach to massage therapy and while I neither relaxed nor enjoyed my life and the human touch for that solid hour, it was my high and evidently unrealistic expectation that let me down, not the magic eight ball (maybe a little). And while I probably should've lowered my expectations and while she should've raised her own bar of excellence a notch or two, I came to find that I went in for a massage but walked out with some great material. It reminds me of that twenty-year period in my life when I was chasing that worship leader dream, and the whole time I had this comedy/writing gig sitting right under my nose. I was so busy setting my sights on this other thing that I missed what God intended it to be—intended ME to be. Maybe it wasn't my day to get the massage of a lifetime, but I got the chapter of a lifetime. It just goes to show you that all things work out the way they're supposed to when we are surrendered to the Lord (Holy Bible–ish). I hope your massage experience turns out better than mine, but if it doesn't, just make it a chapter in your book instead.

CHAPTER 15

THE BABYSITTER
AND THE BIBOPSY

$\mathcal{I}$ feel like this is as good a time as any to let you in on what was quite possibly one of the most terrifying events of my life. It spanned the course of about two weeks. It all started when a friend of mine found a lump on my right breast.

Let me back up.

A friend of mine, WHO IS A NURSE PRACTITIONER, found a lump on my breast in a routine breast exam in a legit doctor's office. I feel like that's good information to have.

So, my friend found this lump and told me she was concerned and wanted me to have it checked out. My mind immediately went worst-case scenario, then to the writing of my will (*Daddy, you get all my bills. End of will.*), then to Aunt Voula in *My Big Fat Greek Wedding*:

"All my life I have a lump in the back of my neck. Right here. Always a lump. Then I start the menopause.

The lump got bigger from the hormonies [pronounced WHORE-MO'-KNEES]. It started to grow. So, I go to the doctor and he did the biop . . . the bop . . . the, the bios . . . the bib . . . the bibopsy. And inside the lump he found teeth and a spinal column. Yes. Inside the lump was my twin."

Lord, why do I have a lump and what is in it? Is it my twin? I've always wished for a sibling, but not this way. Maybe it's a geocache. Please let it be a golden nugget that is removable and redeemable for a trip to the Caymans and a Range Rover with a tan interior. Maybe this isn't so worst-case after all. Maybe this is best-case. Maybe this is what the Powerball really is. What a shame for all these people who have been "playing it" all these years. And here it was, hiding in my breast all along. Who knew.

Please hear me. So many women struggle with the very real, sometimes life-or-death, issue of breast cancer. In no way, shape or form do I take this lightly. It is a serious thing and my heart goes out to every single woman ever affected by it. But also know that if I do not make light of my own ailments and potential problems, I will not make it through life without a padded room, a checkerboard and an imaginary friend.

Because I was due for my yearly girly exam anyway, I decided to be efficient and schedule my Pap smear and my mammogram both on the same day. This would be my first mammogram, so I was a bit apprehensive, yet confident in my ability to turn any awkward situation into . . . a little bit more of an awkward situation. My friends told me that this should be a great day for me since I had been single for four years. After I reminded them of all the ways it was not the same, I kindly asked that they leave the joke-telling to me.

I arrived at the clinic and settled in for my yearly checkup. It was epic as usual, ladies. Always a good time. I got dressed, went upstairs and stripped it down for my mammo. If you've ever had one, you know that what I'm about to say is the God's-honest. This technician pulled and pushed and shoved on my girls till there was nothing left of me. She took my dignity and whatever was left of my B cup. I had to go down a bra size when I left.

She yanked on me so hard that I could've sworn she was trying to milk me. I think I felt let-down for a brief second. I said to her, "Look. You can keep tryin', but my youngest is eleven. You ain't gonna get anything outta there." That was the first time I had ever been milked by anything other than my babies and I gotta say, I was not a fan.

After she got me down to the consistency of two-ply toilet paper, nay, ashes, she was nose to nose with me. "Are you comfortable?" The nerve of her to ask! I said, "Are YOU comfortable? Please say no!" *Goodness gracious alive, lady! Do I look comfortable to you?* My boobs looked like they were waiting to be flipped. They were about to bubble up any second. Luckily, that was the fastest photo shoot I had ever had—she got me in and out before I had to officially rededicate my life to Christ for all the internal curse words running through my heart and mind.

A few days went by when I received a phone call. "Ms. Land, your Pap smear came back abnormal. We need you to come in for a biop . . . the bop . . . the, the bios . . . the bib . . . the bibopsy."

Of course, my Pap smear came back abnormal. I would expect nothing less. And of course, I'll come in. Just let me revise my will. This time I went a little deeper, leaving all my Free People clothes to my friends Tammy and Wendy, and my leather sofa to my friend Heather. It was getting real.

Once again, I had the bright idea to get it all done in one fell swoop. I would go in for the bibopsy and the reading of my mammogram results all on the same day. Ingenious.

Two long weeks later, the day finally arrived. Somewhere along that twenty-minute drive I had an idea. *When I get in the doctor's office, I'm gonna make a video. And I'm gonna call it . . .* THE GYNECOLOGIST.

YESSSSS!!! Surely this was not only brilliance in action, but it would get my mind on something besides my fate that lay ahead.

I got into the room, changed into my backwards nightgown and proceeded with what would, without a doubt, be an award-winning vlog. I took every bit of time allotted to me during my wait, and right as I was wrapping up, there it was—the double tap on the door, followed by the walk-in. *Here he comes, and following closely behind is his little accountability partner— BABYSITTER. She is about as useless as those posters they put up on the ceiling—good for nothing. She doesn't even put on gloves. She's just there to make sure no hanky-panky happens.*

And yes, thank you, ma'am, for being here. What a relief! I was feeling so sexy and ready to make my move. I was so tempted to stumble, but your mere presence has saved this man's marriage and my integrity. You are a hero.

Upon their entrance, I quickly threw my phone over on the chair and got into Pap smear mode. "Go ahead and slide down to the end of the table. A little farther . . . a little farther . . . a little fa . . ." *LOOK, dude!! I am already hanging off the end of the bed. Can you give me a hand, OR TWO? I did not come here to exercise! My legs are quivering so bad I feel like I've been holding a sleeping baby with nothing but my knees. I'm gonna need an escort to my car!*

Once I got in the lateral squatting position, he let out a little laugh. *WHAT?!? You mock me? Oh, no you didn't!! I bathed eight times this morning and shaved three! I also used my Juicy Couture just for you, so don't even!!*

Then, with as much professionalism as he could muster, he said, "Ms. Land. You forgot to take off your underwear."

Seriously? I had one job. In all my independent filmmaking I couldn't even perform my only requirement. Epic fail.

Then he and his little mistress-getter confused me more than my ninth-grade algebra teacher. THEY TURNED AROUND FOR ME TO TAKE OFF MY UNDERWEAR!

I said, "You're turning around?? What kind of sense does that make? You're about to be eye level!"

He found my antics unamusing, but she laughed. *You're welcome, lady. You need some comic relief after having to babysit all day. That's a tough job! I remember.*

The doctor proceeded with my biopsy as I lay on that table for what felt like three and a half years. I watched two seasons of *Grey's Anatomy* while I was there. Every now and then I looked over at Babysitter and asked, "You enjoying the show?" Suddenly, as if he had found a golden ticket, the doctor said, "Ah-ha! I think I found the culprit!"

Culprit?

The culprit?

There's a culprit? And you found it?

Pray tell.

He said, "Well, Ms. Land . . . it looks like you have a zit on your uterus."

A zit, you say?

On my uterus?

A zit . . .

I lay there for a minute (I had nowhere to go), fist to forehead, and I did what I do best. I said the first thing that popped into my head.

"Well . . . CAN YOU POP IT?"

Again with the laughing!! So tired of being mocked, sir, but whatever.

Look, if you have a zit, you pop it. This isn't rocket science. Can you or not?

He said, "Well, no ma'am! That wouldn't be very comfortable for you!"

I said, "In case you were unaware, I'm not very comfortable right now anyway!"

He assured me that in time it would go away and in the meantime, would cause me no pain. So many emotions were running through my being by this point. So many questions.

How in the world do you get a zit on your uterus?

Was he gonna tell anybody?

I felt it was time for a serious conversation after his findings. "Look, Doctor. I'm so glad that's all it is. Really glad!! I'm grateful to be here, but listen. I've got people praying for me, and I'm gonna need you to come up with something better than that! I ain't taking that back to my girlfriends. They will have a field day! I ain't doin' it."

Traumatized but relieved, I got dressed and headed upstairs to get my mammogram results read. One down, one to go. The tech put my X-rays up on the screen and proceeded.

"These two little circles are your breasts."

I said, "Umm, no disrespect, but they weren't little till I came to see YOU two weeks ago. Let's get that straight right now." She continued on, asking the question, "Do you see this white spot on the right breast?" It was about the size of a quarter. Yes, I saw it.

"I don't know how to tell you this without just spitting it out," she continued, "so I'm just gonna say it. That white spot is the lump you were feeling. And that lump is the only bit of elasticity you have left in your breast."

Silence (the awkward kind) . . .

What was that noise? Oh, a pin dropped. Okay.

So, let me get this straight. The lump that you mammogrammed two weeks ago is nothing more than remnants of my former, perkier, pre-baby self? Is that what I'm hearing?

I said, "Well, how 'bout you tell me something I DON'T know! I didn't need a mammo to tell me that!"

She assured me that was all it was—that nothing was

wrong and I would get to continue usage of my clothes and sofa for another day.

And then I said, again, "Look. I'm so glad that's all it is. Really glad!! I'm grateful to be here, but listen. I've got people praying for me, and I'm gonna need you to come up with something better than that! I ain't taking that back to my girlfriends. They will have a field day! I ain't doin' it."

So, basically, I went through two weeks of torment only to walk out with a really bizarre case of adult acne and my eighteen-year-old boob trying to make a comeback.

Shameful.

Thank you, Lord, for a good(ish) report.

Thank you for the opportunity to continue wearing that new Free People sweater.

I left with deep gratitude to be alive and well. I'll take a zit on the uterus any day. I also left with the realization that life is short, it's "but a vapor" (Holy Bible), that I needed to hug my kids a little tighter and that I was gonna have one heck of a chapter if I ever got the chance to write a book (that never crossed my mind). I was also really grateful that Babysitter kept me from making the mistake of a lifetime, since I was ever-so-attracted to a hundred-year-old man who consciously chose eye level as his career. (*Why, sir?*) What a relief!

I'm telling you, after that insane few weeks, I needed

a long bath, some chocolate and some mind-numbing HGTV. Because I would rather die a thousand deaths than to be lying on that pornographic table ever again.

I ain't doin' it . . . (till next year).

———————

Life is full of the scary—the unknown—the what-ifs.

For years, I lived in a constant state of "what if." Even as a child, I would worry myself sick until I had to stay home from school with anxiety. It was and is a real thing and we all deal with it differently. Some of us need greater measures of assurance than others. There is no shame.

I personally am trying to adopt my granny's life motto—DON'T BORROW TROUBLE. IT HAS ENOUGH OF ITS OWN. (My granny also likes to quote the Holy Bible with a twist.) But she, and the gospel of Matthew, are right. It has taken me years to get this through my thick head and I still struggle. What good does worry do? It's probably the reason my hair is so thin and I had to get extensions for six months. Worry has sucked more joy and brain cells from my life than fifteen years of bad marriage. And I don't know about you, but I'm over it. I'm tired of allowing it to rob me of peace and fun and happiness. I'm not saying that situations aren't attention-worthy. They are. That two-week run of the unknown had me shaking. I wonder how much more peaceful it could've been if it had me trusting.

CHAPTER 16

TATTOOS, REBELLION AND DIRTY NEEDLES

When I was growing up, tattoos were taboo and rebellious. My dad cringed at the thought of his daughter reaching to shake hands with his boss, only to show off a nautical star she branded on her hand during a night of what could only have been pure and utter insanity. Luckily, no nautical stars ever left their mark, but he did threaten me on more than one occasion should I ever be so inclined to walk the lonely road of body art. Today, tattoos are widely recognized as a definitive, creative way for people to express themselves and tell their stories. And depending on said tattoo, they are also recognized as lame, beautiful, hideous, symbolic, impulsive and/or intriguing. I've heard it all. As we well know, everybody has an opinion.

Some tattoos have meaning. Others only symbolize the fact that you were barely coherent when you got yours. You know who you are . . .

I, for one, love a little marking every now and again. Mine are nothing elaborate or anything to write home about. I'm not trying to be hard or cool or Kat Von D over here. I'm just a wannabe. I got my first tattoo when I was thirty. I knew for my first one it had to be perfect, so naturally, being from the South, I went with a beautiful cursive monogram with the initials of my then-husband and my still-two-children. The letters read *NBA*—something I didn't think all the way through. Also, I am now divorced, so there's that. Still, I don't regret it. It marks a time in my life and it's small enough that most people don't even notice. Luckily, my dad's name also starts with a *B*, so if people do ask, I can always say that middle initial stands for Bud. I'm also on the lookout for my next husband's name to start with a *B*. It just makes sense, so if you know of anybody . . .

My second tattoo, purchased around age thirty-three, reads *Psalm 121* on my left wrist (pronounced SALM, not PALM). You can read it for yourself, but a sweet reminder to me that my help comes from above.

Still, some of you hate tattoos and are probably judging me right now. It's okay. I still love you. Tiny pieces of any respect that my parents have for me get chipped away with every single one I get.

"What are you gonna do when you get old??"

"Well . . . I guess I'll just be cool and old."

This answer never seems to suffice. Although I'm fairly certain that by the time I'm "old" there will be a cream that gently washes away any remnants of bad ink jobs. But if not, it's fine. We can agree to disagree. Either way, my third tattoo is a terrible story, so don't leave now.

Here's how it went down. I was out with some of my oldest and dearest friends on my thirty-sixth birthday. We lived in Colorado Springs at the time, so downtown Denver was the place to be. I had just finished reading a book by Ann Voskamp called *One Thousand Gifts*. My depiction and takeaway of this writing cannot do it justice, so I won't even try. Just let it be known that I was so moved by this book that I was willing to stamp my body with permanent ink to prove it. I wanted to add a tiny black string around my finger to remind me "in all things, be grateful." So off we go. And down we go. Literally. Underground. Downtown Denver. To Frank. Frank was a novelty—an eccentric. Why I thought this was a good idea, I'll never know. Frank spoke of many things—mostly shenanigans. And I listened intently as he prepared what could've very well been a dirty needle (I'm still not sure). I listened and listened until I could no longer hear the words that were coming out of his mouth. For you see, I could hear nothing over my sudden, intense pain, comparable only to the enlightening stage of childbirth. The ring of fire (but liter-

ally, the "string" of fire). I had no idea I was even pregnant, but this baby was about to come out the tip of my
right ring finger. And he was a big one.

"I'm sorry, Frank. Excuse me. Do you have an anes-
thesiologist on hand, because I'm pretty sure I'm gonna
need an epidural for this. It may only be a little ink, but
sir, if I didn't know better I'd say you're sawing off my
digit. Kindly stop lest I die." I'm not kidding. I thought
my time was up at thirty-six—underground—with Frank.
*Don't let me go this way, Lord. It wasn't worth it and
I'm not ready.*

One very expensive trip to the ER later and the results were conclusive. Frank cut me nearly to the bone
and left me with what looks nothing like a string—more
like a Halloween spider that I endearingly named Charlotte. She's really a beautiful addition. I think I got that
tattoo to remind me of something, but I can't for the life
of me remember what it was (something about being
grateful, maybe). Because now all I think about when I
see it is FRANK. Thanks, Frank. You're always in my
heart. And on my finger (but hey, at least I still have one).
And at least I'm not the only one walking around with a
bad ink job. Some of you have it way worse than I do.
I've seen the work. My condolences.

I digress.

Back to the topic at hand.

I do not claim to be a theologian on the matter of permanent body ink. I just like getting tattoos at random. To each his own.

Many people ask me about the tattoo on my right arm, so let me give you a brief what-for. Besides trying to make my parents extremely proud, I wanted to get something symbolic of the valley I had just crawled my way out of. Also, after Frank, I needed redemption.

Here's the story:

After my divorce, I had to learn how to do life again. I was flying blind into this new season of new life, but I was hopeful. We—me and my two children—were hurting but strong. And we were headed in this new direction together.

And we were gonna make it, Lord willing and the creek don't rise. I was determined.

For some reason I loved arrows (they're all the rage) and as luck would have it, upon my study of them, I found that they are a symbol of strength and direction.

While one arrow can be easily broken, a bundle is tougher to break. And here we were—this little bundle of weak strength. Being held tight by the arrow-maker Himself.

Figuring it out.

Forging a path.

Walking a new direction.

Together.

After lots of Pinteresting and careful consideration of where body marking #4 would actually take place, I gave it a go on Birthday #41.

NO RAGRETS. (Please see Google on the inter-web for further explanation of this spelling.)

Three "arrows" headed in the same direction.

This stupid, ridiculous, sweet, symbolic, beautiful (whatever you want to call it) piece of ink tells a part of my story. It forever and always reminds me that we are strong. I remember where I've been and where I'm headed.

I remember starting over. I may not be what some would consider a highly intelligent individual. Sometimes things are hard for me to piece together. I suck at math, and most of the time can't remember who won which wars or where the children of Israel were exiled from. When it was time for me to walk through the divorce, I knew nothing about the family judicial system and I could not afford an attorney. So, do you know what I did? The local courthouse offered free assistance from an attorney for fifteen minutes a week for those of us who could not afford one. We could ask any question we could think of and receive his or her help for that set amount of time. So, I went to the courthouse for months and I spoke with that attorney for fifteen minutes every single week. I took that paperwork week after week, correcting mistake after mistake, until I got it right. I went to my friend Heather's house, and I spread that paperwork out on her floor and googled the crap out of some legal terms. I signed and I paid the fees and I asked the questions and I felt overwhelmed and scared, but I did not quit. And on one of the hardest days of my life, Divorce Day, I stood there in front of that judge, still knowing nothing about family law, but having done it on my own. I did it weak and afraid, but I did it.

It was a long few months. I cried many tears and screamed at the injustice my kids and I were walking through. But I also walked away saying, "Good grief, girl. Look what you just did. You made it out alive." Over the next several months I watched as my children struggled to put the pieces back together, and I struggled just the same, knowing that I had a hand in their hurt. I saw them walk through misunderstanding and heartache, and I watched them be brave earlier than they should've had to be. I watched us move slowly uphill, grabbing limbs and digging in our heels and taking the hands of the ones who were continuing to pull us up. We were moving forward. I saw it with my own eyes. Me and my little arrows.

There are things they may not understand and there has been heartache along the way, but I pray that they walk their journey knowing who I am and who I'm raising them to be. Tenacious. Tough and tender and full of grit.

Our story is not over. God is not finished with us yet. My team of three. We are still making it.

And you know what? Maybe I AM rebelling. Rebelling against all of the naysayers and the things that say I can't do it, that I won't make it. Rebelling against complacency—against the hurdles, the hard places, the status quo.

I am finding, as I meet new people and hear their stories, that I am not the only one walking that road. Many of us are facing or have faced circumstances we never asked for or imagined being in—where we have to keep moving. We are all learning that even in the weak places we are still strong. And we are going forward—together. Because we are meant to walk it out together. I could never run my race without my cheerleaders from the sidelines. Without the ones telling me I can do it and I can finish well.

And you can finish well, too. Whatever hard road you're walking, you can do it. You are stronger than you even know. I know you are wearing a lot of hats, and I know you're tired, but don't quit. Whatever that thing is that is staring you in the face, stare back. Tell it to take a seat and watch you work. Because I promise you this: if you will lean in and let God take your hand and lead you up that hard road, you will stand on the other side the victor. Your side-hustle attorneying will pay off, and you will be able to stand in front of whatever judge there is on your journey and say, "I'm here. I'm present. I'm fighting for justice. I'm fighting for hearts. Me. I did this."

And when you're done with that chapter, whatever it may be, tell the story. Tell other people about what you went through. Show them how strong you were and how weak you were and how you wanted to quit but didn't. Tell them about how you cried and you screamed and you did your own paperwork even though you could barely spell "judicial" and you were heartbroken. Tell them how you felt like a horrible parent and you begged God to let your kids just be okay. Tell the world, because I promise you somebody in your wake is going through their own living nightmare. Somebody you know needs your story. Tell it. Let it be a gift of strength that you offer to them, and to yourself—a gift that pushes you up that last leg of the race. Because we are in this together.

Show them your scars. Show them your arrows. And tell them that if you can make it, so can they. Rebel against your own insecurity that draws you back and tells you that your contribution isn't important. Rebel against the person who doesn't want you to share because of shame. Stand up for truth and stand up for the story. Be brave. You've got something to say. Let the words of your pages and the reading of your book relieve tears and remedy the weariness of your soul. Your vulnerability will bring inspiration, not shame—and it will quiet the lies that whisper to the hearts of people everywhere telling them they will not make it.

Yes, they will.

Yes, you will.

Tell your self-doubt to take a seat as you stand up and read the intro to your greatest work—your autobiography.

Leave a legacy. Be a rebel.

CHAPTER 17

IT TAKES A VILLAGE

*I*f I've said it once, I've said it a thousand times—I never meant to be a comedienne. I know what you're thinking. "Come on, Heather. Haven't you always been funny?" The short answer? Of course, people. Always. But only in private. Only for those truly in the inner circle. Or at parties. Or in awkward situations. Or boring situations. Or in long lines at the grocery store. Okay, so basically most of my life and in any situation. But still, the thought of touring the country in a bus and standing on a stage telling jokes?

No to that.

That said, you couldn't peel me away from this new-found career if you tried. I love all that my stupid videos have afforded me. I actually love stand-up. There, I said it. I love being pushed out on the stage night after night, coffee cup in hand, gum in mouth, and being told to knock 'em dead. I love the fear and the nerves and the unknown of standing in front of a different crowd every night. A crowd whose roaring laughter could potentially boost my ego to heights unseen or whose deafening silence could send me into a clinical depression with a side of binge eating for the win. I just never know. But that's part of the thrill. The thrill of the not-knowing. And the feeling of actual certainty that I'm doing what I'm meant to do far outweighs the fear of failure. The fear of the unknown is actually the drive.

The gratification is in the risk, and it's in the payoff that comes in the form of laughter and stories of heartache and redemption . . . from you. When we talk after the shows or when you comment on my videos. That's the payoff. It's in the travel and the exploration and in telling my children I went for it. It's in not looking back, in the vision of what's to come. It's in new relationships and a new way of life. It's in embracing the unfamiliar until it feels like the norm. And this . . . this is my norm.

Let's get one thing straight before we move on. Bus life is not for everyone, but it's definitely for me. Going down the road for fifteen hours at a time on a moving, New York City-loft-sized apartment that is carrying ten other passengers along with it, strangely enough, makes me about as happy as a pig in squalor. Waking up to, working all day with and going to sleep to the same people day in and day out makes my heart skip a beat.

If you ever decide to take to road life, there are some

important facts for you to know. Choose your bunk wisely. The gentle, harsh hum of the motor will absolutely lull you to sleep on the bottom bunk. That's my first choice. Just make sure nobody's around to watch you roll out of it in the mornings. It's not a good look for anybody. The middle bunk is easiest to get in and out of in my personal opinion and could potentially create a most euphoric feeling of claustrophobia, seeing as how you are surrounded by walls and bodies on every side. The top bunk sways, so that is strictly reserved for those ranking low on the age totem pole, i.e. interns. (Sorry, girls.)

A few more good pieces of information to have: Always choose the game that you're good at when traveling with competitive people. Make sure everyone gets a turn when choosing songs; and do engage in impromptu dance parties hosted by your dancing-fool production manager who thinks he's Bruno Mars. You will not regret it. Also, do make friends with your bus driver, do learn to eat dinner at midnight, and don't, under any circumstances, "use the bathroom" when you're using the bathroom. All of this is pertinent to enjoying life on the road.

There are also great perks to road life OFF the bus. Like stepping foot into a different theater on the nightly. Learning its smells, its sounds, its aura. Feeling out the room and breathing it in is one of my favorite things, next to bubble baths and mimosas.

I wish you could be with me right now. I snuck away to the balcony of a venue where I'm performing in Charlotte, North Carolina. I'm watching part of my team set the stage. They use big words I don't understand and they do techy things with cords they call cables and screens and pulleys and lights, and it makes me feel stupid. They tear black tape and they move speakers and they check the sound on my piano with more playing ability in their little fingers than I have in my whole body. I use my hands to type words, but they use their hands to make those words come alive on the stage night after night.

Before I found my way to the nosebleeds earlier today, I was surrounded by the rest of my tour team in a creative meeting. So many beautiful minds going in so many different directions, but coming together in the end for one cause, one goal. I feel certain that given a mic and a cup of coffee, any one of them could also stand up there and do a little comedy while they're at it, but that may be asking too much.

The misconception of tour life viewed through the lens of social media is that it's this one-man show, but most of you know better. To some of you it would seem effortless. How hard could it be, right? It's who you are. Just get up there and hold that mic and be funny and sing us a few songs. But how many times do I have to tell you? Being a comedienne is not some secret career path

I've always hoped to follow. It's not a craft I've been hon-
ing for the past decade. I haven't been hitting the comedy
clubs in between nursing my children and fixing dinner. I
never signed up for comedy. You did. You signed me up.
You told me I could do it, so I did . . . and here we are.
Just a few short months ago I had to figure this thing out.
Am I going to keep working my big-girl job or am I
going to sit across the dinner table from my daddy and
tell him I'm quitting my job to do comedy full-time? Am
I going to give up the only bit of security and stability
I've ever known to take a risk based on the popularity of
a few videos and some blogs?

Actually, yes.

I think that's exactly what I'm going to do.

And so I am.

But I'm not doing it alone. Were it not for the consistent encouragement of a few close friends and family
members, and now, my tour family, I would be curled up
in the fetal position in the corner of a room somewhere
eating checkers and talking to my imaginary friend. The
fear and the weight and the responsibility is gripping and
can numb your mind quicker than gin on an empty stomach, but do you know what I'm finding?

I'm finding that the payoff is greater than the risk.
The possibility of a downfall, in my humble opinion, is
way more palatable than the question of what-if.

And the team around me that spurs me on and loves

me and the behind-the-scenes payoff as much as I love hugging necks and telling jokes is worth the ride. Can I introduce you to my road family? Will you indulge me? I promise these people are worth your while.

Chandy—Producer of "all the things." She is a beast. She believes and she pushes and she invests. She makes the tour happen in the first place. She is intelligent and caring and hilarious. She is the mama, the big sister, the driving force. I knew the first time I ever talked to her that she was the one. I finally put a ring on it and am hopeful for a lifelong marriage. Me and Chandy.

Ray—Tour manager—a lover AND a fighter. He takes care of all things from ticketing to catering. Ray is our real-life tour teddy bear in five-foot, seventeen-inch form who puts up with more shenanigans than he would probably care to disclose.

Chrissy—but I call her Brooke. Brookie heads up merch and oversees our *I Ain't Doin' It* interns on the road. She is no-nonsense, takes no crap, is my equal in the sarcasm department and has endless knowledge about most subjects in the known world. But don't let her fool you. I've seen her shed a tear or two. She is creative and funny and she's a go-getter . . . and I get her.

Elisabeth and Bekah—our interns. These girls keep us young. They are all things life and love, fun and flirty. They are crowd pleasers and full of low-key innocence and potential. When I'm around them, I don't know about you, but I'm feeling twenty-two.

Stephen—If Stephen plays his cards right, there's a possibility he'll make Book #2. Until then, just know that he is my production manager on the road. He pushes buttons and does hard work and heavy lifting. He oversees sound, lighting and video at every venue where we perform. He wears a headset and says things like, "Stand by. Spotlight to pick her up on Stage Left. Fade music. And go." He is brilliant and kind, funny and caring, and he knows his music like I know jokes. He also genuinely laughs at all my jokes night after night, which is precisely why he got a few extra sentences in this chapter. I mean, maybe that's not the only reason. I digress . . .

Pepper—Coach, program director, seasoned actor. My Yoda—he guides with class and poise. He keeps me in time and gently threatens my life if I go ten minutes over, one. more. time.

Amy V.—Executor. List maker, box checker, sender of thorough emails. She makes sure the *i*'s are dotted and *t*'s are crossed, but make no mistake, she is also singing musical tunes at the top of her lungs during our late-night listening parties. Turn on some *Rent* and she lights up like a Christmas tree.

Tosha—Tosha is . . . That's it. She just is. She has been my friend for twenty-five years and continues to be that above all things. Above every disagreement, above every accolade and reward. She is my constant companion and a source of contentment on and off the road. She is stage manager, assistant, horrible dancer. She is off-key singer, avid reader and lover of all people. She is the contact for all my shows and she is the emergency contact for my children on every form. She is married to my business partner, the person who helped get this thing off the ground and my big brother of sorts, Russ, and the two of them together help make my business and personal worlds go 'round.

Jami, APG, JoJo, Leslie, Christiana, and Brenda—My extended family off-road. To you these are just names, but to me, they are all vital pieces of the road-life puzzle. They keep me on the right flight on the right day and they keep those spreadsheets clean and coming. (If only I knew how to read them!) From advance work to logistics, they keep this machine oiled and the wheels turning. They are life support to each and every one of us who spend night after night on the road and away from home. Actually, scratch that. The road. This IS my home. And these people make up my village.

Our village.

And our village is strong. Fixed. Our homes are made up of bunks on a bus, but our hearts are a settlement. We are guided by the same principles. Centered. We are all of different bends and trades, but we function as a unit. We are all of equal value. Our walls are strong. We work hard and we love well and we live for justice and we fight hard for the good of the whole. We are unified.

These are my allies—they push and they spur and they steer the ship. These people—a group that I never saw coming. My family has expanded. Now I also come home to a bus full of people who equally believe in me and in the cause and in the grind. They believe in the vision and they believe that what we are doing matters—that there is purpose in the laughter and the story. And this family of mine wasn't even my family a year ago, but from here on out, we are tied. And I want to be tied. In a world that tells us we can do all the things alone, the truth is, we just need people. We need community. Cheerleaders—telling us to go after the thing and do it afraid. Lovers of the ride who tell us, "If you don't, you'll regret it." Motivators who say, "You'll never know until you try." Believers who remind you, "I have faith in you."

Friends . . . fans . . . you . . . who love and encourage and keep the dream alive. We all need each other.

We don't all, however, need life on the road. It's not for everyone, but it's most definitely for me. Not everybody can sleep well nights on end in a moving vehicle. Even some in our team struggle. Me? I sleep like a baby. I always choose the bottom passenger-side bunk. The hum of the motor lulls me to sleep on the nightly, as soon as I'm able to wind down . . . which is usually around

2:00 A.M. I pull that curtain and curl up in that pitch-black coffin-like cocoon and rest like I haven't in years . . . until the bus driver hits a pothole . . . or runs over those lines on the side of the road that sound like death is near. Or until he slams on the brakes and my body is thrust into tomorrow. Still, though, I sleep like a nursing home patient.

It's also a good thing I love the people I travel with. If not, life would be miserable, as our "living room" comfortably fits less than all of us. We somehow cram ourselves in night after night for charades, musical guessing games and long chats where we solve the world's problems while eating too much. If and when road life is up for me, I may just purchase a motor home and re-create this whole scene myself. I'll just bring my whole team and travel around doing comedy shows at local KOAs. It won't be exactly the same, but maybe a close second.

Just kidding. I ain't doin' it. But I am gonna ride it out (pun intended) as long as life lets me. I'm gonna enjoy my tribe and my life, and hopefully when I'm sleeping for real in my nursing home village I'll be able to tell stories of this village and how these people have impacted my life.

May your village be as strong as this one.

CHAPTER 18

HOLIDAYS

*I*t's a million degrees in my beloved hometown right now, and summer hasn't even begun. I'm already over the weather and showing the world my arms, so I'm just gonna move it right along. In my head, it's already fall. I love everything about fall—pumpkin spice lattes; pumpkin spice teas; pumpkin spice candles; pumpkin spice breads, vegetables, body wash . . . you name it. Just kidding. Not really . . . but kinda (I draw the line at pumpkin spice deodorant). But let's get real—everything is laced with pumpkin and spice. If they made pumpkin spice markers, I would sniff them. I know what you're thinking: "But you made a video making fun of people who love pumpkin spice!" Yes. Yes, I did. And many of my videos are making fun of myself, much like that one. Because I can't lie, won't lie—I'm a pumpkin spice fan. And look, I'm just gonna say it. If you don't love fall and everything that comes with it (college football), I question your salvation. I'm pretty sure heaven smells like fall. And I'm pretty sure that when Hobby Lobby puts their fall and Christmas décor out for the masses, I'm checking out of real life.

One thing I'm not looking forward to, however, is my annual coughing-up-a-lung bronchitis/sinus infection/ walking pneumonia trifecta. Last year I hung onto that triple threat with all my might for a solid six months. SIX (6). Six months of getting swabbed and poked and x-rayed and rubbing essential oils on my big toe and barking like a dog in the middle of church. I for real bruised my ribs, you guys. But seriously, there has got to be a better way to see if I have strep or the flu than to stick that giant needle-of-a-Q-tip up my nose and down my throat. Not only do they literally take a piece of my sinuses, but they take a piece of my dignity every single time. Forever traumatized.

And is that not the longest five seconds of your life??

Last time I had it done, I actually went home, took a nap, baked a cake and recovered from all my sickly conditions while they were still swabbing me. Like, draw a gallon of blood, cut off my fingernails, waterboard me— anything but the swab. And at least YouTube that junk so we can make some money off it. Somebody should at least reap the benefits of this heinous procedure. Like, please make sure you grab a shot of me gagging as I'm white-knuckling the arm of my seat. Don't leave that out. If they would only make a pumpkin spice nasal spray, maybe, just maybe, I could make it through my physical dysfunction without hating life. (Get on that, somebody. It's all you.)

Fingers crossed this year is different. I don't know if I can handle it again. Sickness and single-mom life mix like eggs and ketchup. (Some of y'all need to quit doing that. I digress . . .)

All this to say, I love the end of the year far more than I like the middle. There are some major holidays that are not particularly my favorites, but I pass through them with a smile to get to the good stuff. One of those being Halloween.

If you are a lover of all things horrifying, don't hate. To each his own. I for one struggle mostly with people's random, nonsensical choice of costume. Not only do I not need for my youngest child to have nightmares till she's twenty-five, I also don't need to be explaining to my children why we can see all your pixie dust—there, Tinkerbell. And hey there, Sexy Skeleton. We can see a little bit more than just your bones, girlfriend. I'll stop. Let's move on to the fact that grown folks try to come to your door to get candy, all in the name of their two-week-old child they're pushing around in a stroller. Your child is still nursing, ma'am. And we have a four-tooth minimum at this house, okay? That goes for you, too, seventy-five-year-old granddaddy. Your grandchild is not in the car. I'm not stupid. All this to say, I could skip it altogether.

I look forward to most of the major calendar events of the year. I don't, however, look forward to Tax Free Weekend or Black Friday.

I would rather die a thousand deaths than step foot inside a commercial establishment on Tax Free Weekend. I know . . . I'm in the minority. Most of my girlfriends are all giddy at the possibility of saving $5.32 at checkout. I would rather lose a limb (truth) and give up sugar for a year (lie) than brave the retail elements on this annual nightmare weekend. I WOULD RATHER PAY THE TAX than have to fight you over that last pack of #2 pencils. You can have 'em, lady. No, really. You go right ahead. Because I can promise you by the look on your face, they mean more to you than they ever will to me. My kids will live with one pack of twenty-five. I'm willing to risk them being publicly shamed and humiliated in front of their peers on the first day of school so that you can walk away the victor. Actually, I need to thank you for knocking a whopping $4 off my already $312 shopping bill. Go and be blessed.

Y'all. Seriously. I cannot even deal. It is the mirror image of Black Friday minus the sweater weather and all the feels. I need to be holding a Starbucks and listening to Christmas music on the loudspeaker if I'm gonna go through all this nonsense. I could ALMOST MAYBE go to blows with you over that last three-ring binder if we weren't both dripping sweat and exhausted from all seven of your children who, for some reason unbeknownst to me, you bring with you shopping on the worst weekend of the year. Explain yourself . . .

I mean, you know you're miserable. It's written all over your face (in eight dry-erase markers and twenty-four colored pencils). I'm miserable, too. Your kids are making me miserable for the both of us. And you're about to snap. I see you eyeing that pharmacy. You're about to go grab something to take the edge off. Do it. I'll watch the kids. And grab me something while you're at it.

You people . . . WHY?? Black Friday is just as bad. Not only do you mow people over for a bed-in-a-bag and a set of wooden spoons, but you map that mess out. You spend days looking at circulars and crafting your routes. And I know that some of you live for this moment and it is endearing and bonding and all the things you say it is, but why in Lord's name you would rather stay up all night and waste precious shut-eye while your small children are asleep I will never know. And I haven't even mentioned your mental fortitude to fight with ruthless, cutthroat patrons who will go down swinging for a sixty-five-inch. There is no Dutch oven or toolbox worth all that, in my opinion. Some of you, though, swear by it, live for it and even come out smiling when it's over. Good for you. Black Friday heroes. You win. Some of y'all are more concerned about your earnings than you are the actual representation of Thanksgiving. You're praying over Thanksgiving dinner, grateful that Aunt Linda came to town, but have no qualms wrestling her to the ground on Aisle 3 in Target for a griddle. You're gonna get it, right now, even if you have to lose your digits and your dignity in the process.

Despite my disdain for competitive shopping, I love the holidays and all that comes with them.

Christmas in my family was always a sweet time. I was an only child on a road full of old people, so their Christmas always revolved around coming over Christmas morning to see my gifts. I was a sweet child who loved Jesus and people and I, even at a young age, had a heart for the less privileged, but let's not get crazy. I also loved E.T. and Little Orphan Annie and if I had not gotten that T-shirt and that locket, I most certainly would've cried real tears. My desire for a Cabbage Patch Kid and a pink jam box superseded my will to live and my parents knew it. They went to great lengths to hide my gifts, because they knew I was looking. To this day, I love surprises, but I love figuring them out ahead of time even more.

My bedroom was at the very end of a very short hall in our very small house. One year on Christmas Eve, my parents went to great lengths. They got one of their friends to dress as Santa, come into our house late that night and make enough noise for me to wake up and find him putting presents under the tree. I will never forget it. I was mesmerized and perplexed and infatuated with the now 100 percent knowledge that he was forever real. I knew it. Until I didn't.

Jig was up. But when? Not till fifth grade. Another day I will never forget. A conversation involving myself and some of my little girlfriends immediately turned to Christmas, and as I went on to speak of Santa and my excitement for his gifts that coming year—their words mixed with their mocking laughter still ring out like in slow mo—they said, "SANTA ISN'T REAL . . ."

Uhh . . . say what? "You still believe in Santa? Heather!" I was horrified, embarrassed and hurt. Not by Santa not being real. By my parents who let me look like a dang fool all the way to fifth grade. I could've handled it, ya know! Tell a sister! I was such a late bloomer in many senses of the word, but that takes the cake.

Still, I remained a fan of the season and of the euphoric feels that come along with it, year after year. Not only did I look forward to coin rings and baby dolls, but every year on Christmas night, we would always get together with my aunt, uncle and cousins. Every year my uncle would read weird books and quote random facts and make us laugh, while my aunt, who I consider more a mother and one of my favorite people to date, would run around with my mom and granny and set out plates and heat up food, and my cousins and I—we would laugh and sing. Every year for as long as I can remember, my uncle would lead us in a life-changing rendition of "Blue Christmas," and then the true musicianship of every single member of my family would take center stage in the form of Christmas solos. My extended family is a picture of musical beauty, and their voices blended together singing about Jesus and silver bells makes me teary just thinking about it. Christmas also consisted of driving around town looking at Christmas lights—one of my dad's favorite things to do at the holidays.

Ahh . . . all the pretty Christmas lights. Some are as beautiful as a bride on her wedding day. Others . . . straight-up ratchet. You know who you are. I'll never have to buy a ticket to a sideshow again for the rest of my life if you'll just keep 'em lit year 'round.

Looking at Christmas lights wasn't that big of a deal, in my opinion, especially since half the county kept theirs up year 'round anyway. And they still do. And not just my county—your county, too! You know it's the truth. I travel all over the place and everywhere I go, I can promise you, somebody in that town still has their lights up, and some, for the win, still have a bow on the door. What, even . . .

Christmas lights nowadays are mesmerizing to me,

and not because they're beautiful or because they're Christmas lights—but because some of the scenes you people paint in your front yards got me turning sideways like I'm looking at some kindergarten artwork. I feel like I'm looking at that sketch and having to figure out if it's a woman or an old man. It's like that first episode of *Here Comes Honey Boo Boo*—you just can't look away. You might miss something. I drive by some of your houses during the holidays and look for the ticket booth and the cotton candy. I've never tried fried butter, but I feel sure you could sell it by the pound if you'd just start selling tickets. Good grief, this is better than seeing Cirque du Soleil live in Vegas. Could you run in the house and make me a funnel cake while I just sit here and watch? I'm spellbound. I don't wanna miss a thing. Hey kids, forget Disney. We're coming to the Joneses' house every night for a week. It's way better than the Parade of Lights.

Some of you go to Walmart for lights and come home with *a* light. ONE light. That strobe light I talked to you about before—the one that "Daddy" bought. It shoots up a dimly lit spiderweb of lights onto your house, creating the illusion that you give two craps, but falling short by a long shot. Laziness in a box. Others of you have what looks more like a slaying than a sleigh. Y'all are over here mixing scenes from the Holy Bible and *Rudolph* and *National Lampoon's Christmas Vacation*.

You know what really tips the scale for me year after year? Giant Snoopy in a snow globe? No. The drive-thru nativity? Nope.

The light-up Santa Claus leaning over baby Jesus in the manger. WHAT, EVEN?!?!? I am absolutely awe-struck by this holy wonder! I recently saw one of these monstrosities in someone's yard and had to just stop and gawk. They probably thought I was casing their house, but I could not peel my eyes away. My brain is fairly de-mented, so here's how the conversation went with myself in my head:

What is he saying? What is Santa saying to baby Jesus right now? Is he welcoming Him into the world? You know Jesus was here first, right, Santa? I mean, you're not even real. Are you asking Him what He wants for Christmas?

"Dear eight-pound, six-ounce newborn infant Jesus . . ." Are you asking Him if He's been naughty or nice? You know He's not naughty, right? He's Jesus.

And what is Jesus saying back? If I were baby Jesus, I would say something like this:

"Look, Ricky Bobby. I may only be five minutes old, lying here in my golden fleece diaper, but you know I've been around awhile, right? God the Father, Son and Holy Spirit? You've heard of me. Okay, great. So first, I'm gonna need you to back up out of my personal space. And secondly, I'm gonna need you to quit stealing my

thunder. It's my birthday, not yours. Please and thank you. Good-bye. Also, you're not even real."

This whole conversation is disturbing. I know. I'm so sorry. So scary . . . I even had this conversation out loud at a show last year and told a room full of children that Santa wasn't real. Not my finest hour. Anyway, all that nonsense led me to start thinking about some of the ridiculousness that I, myself, bring to Jesus. Now, He loves me. He's Jesus—patient, kind, loving Jesus. But I wonder if He gets tired of my cynical, self-centered requests? I wonder if He gets tired of my talking to Him like He's a genie in a bottle? Of course, He never gets tired of us. But we do it sometimes, don't we? We throw up requests like it's a grown-up Christmas list.

"Lord, I know You're busy with real problems and lots of other broken things to fix, but if You could please miraculously change the attitude of my teenager by Friday I would be most appreciative. I will give extra in the offering on Sunday and I will look for one extra person to tell about You in the line at the grocery store. Yours truly, Tired Mom."

"Jesus, look. Here's the deal. Tennessee football is really struggling this year. If You could help us out, we would sure be obliged. Signed, Volunteer for Life. GBO!"

"Heavenly Father, we thank Thee for all Thy many blessings. While You're up there blessing folks, would You mind causing my sister-in-law, Irma, to come down with the stomach bug so we can just have a peaceful Christmas for once? I know You love her, but Lord . . . well . . . we don't. So, please find it in Yourself to grant me this one wish. If You do, I will never cuss again. Signed, Desperate."

How often do we bring our requests to Jesus as though He is up there with a notepad—"You want what? Hang on and let me grab a pen . . . Okay! Got it!" Or, how often do we come timid and afraid?

God wants to give us good gifts. He is our Father. To this day, my earthly father still loves to give me gifts—to see me happy. He gets tears in his eyes when he sees me light up about something that brings me true joy and fulfillment. How much more does our Heavenly Father delight in giving us good gifts!

We don't have to come to Him like He is the granter of three wishes and only three. There is no having to choose your wishes wisely. There is no tiptoeing. There is no bargaining or bribing. There is no tit-for-tat with Jesus. There's no fear. Make your requests known to God. He sees and hears. And He knows what we need before we do. We do not have to panic, nor do we have to tread softly. We come like a child to a father—boldly and with confidence that He wants to give us beauty in its time. We come trusting that He knows best (the struggle is real). We come to God, our Father—giver of wonderful things. His gifts are so much better than Santa's (but I don't know how anybody's prayer could beat Ricky Bobby's . . .).

This year and every year, I hope the holidays are kind to you and that you are kind to each other. Please don't hurt each other over the last Britney Spears fragrance collection set or the last *Duck Dynasty* sleeping bag, okay? It's not worth all that. Go in peace. At least until the next time you have to buy #2 pencils. (I ain't doin' it.)

CHAPTER 19

KRISPY KREME AND MENTHOLS

The good ol' New Year's resolution—or as I like to call it, The List of Broken Promises. The List of Good Intentions. You know, those things we say we're gonna do but usually don't.

Quit smoking menthols.

No more Krispy Kreme.

Go skydiving.

Take the trip.

Some of us, however, set the bar so extremely low that there is no way on God's green earth we could fail if we tried. Some of you vowed to drop your gym membership this year—a goal that I feel is easily attainable. Well done, you. Others of us shoot for something a little more beyond our reach—something that seems within our grasp but that we just can't quite wrap our fingers around. We get to day three and call it good.

It's too hard. I'm over it. I didn't really need to quit smoking anyway.

You know you do it—"commitment" with no follow-through. Yes, there are those chosen few who actually say they will and they do. To you, sir/ma'am, my hat's off. Your word was your bond. You're the unsung hero. The champion. The victor. You made it. You win.

But for the rest of us . . . Why do we even bother?

Don't beat yourself up. For years, I promised myself to lose twenty pounds. Somewhere around pound ten (more like day ten) and a six-count of Krispy Kreme, I would give up and give in. My will for sugar usually wins out over that size down in jeans. Then . . . oh, brother. Here it comes—self-deprecation for the remaining balance of the calendar year. As if January first is the magic number.

Here's the bottom line—if I wanted to do it, I would, no matter the month or the year.

Because of my history of failure regarding this subject and specific day of the year, New Year's resolutions aren't something I normally commit to, and I most certainly don't hinge the success of my future on them. When I get ready to lose the weight or do the thing, I always do. However, ironically enough, I find myself entering this new year with much resolve. Courses of action have been taken.

"No, seriously this time, Heather. You've got to get

some weight off. You have to go to the gym. It's non-optional. And now is as good a time as any—the new year."

For once, I was right. So off I went.

Starting January first, I got up at 4:30 every single morning and filled that water bottle to the brim and put on that Under Armour. And every single morning I braved the cold and the wind to get in there and make an absolute fool of myself day after stinkin' day. I gave it all I had, which wasn't much. I worked and I sweated and I got on that treadmill and I did those box jumps until that one day.

When I didn't.

I don't know what happened—except that all this talk of me being a non-athlete really is true. With all my might I jumped up onto that box . . . except that I missed the box. I just couldn't quite make the distance. My feet slipped and down I went—right there in front of the 5:00 A.M. crowd and the wall-to-wall mirror that mocked my attempt. Not only did I want to throw up, but I wanted to die a thousand deaths.

Just leave me here. Let me be alone. Let me grieve the death of the box jump in my own way, in my own time. I will move on when I'm ready, and also when the crowd thins out and moves over to the weight room.

I finally got the mental fortitude to brave the shame and pull myself together. I stood up and decided to go out on a good note. If I could get in one solid box jump, I could possibly redeem myself and what's left of my memory at this gym. Make no mistake, after this epic fail, I would only be a memory, because I would, in fact, not be returning. With all my might, I jumped on that box for the final win. I stood on top of that box like a king on a hill and I exited on that day knowing that I went out having conquered that thing, but that I, most assuredly, would always be remembered as the girl who missed it.

That was my last day at the gym. I wish I could erase that solid two weeks of torture from my memory, but every month I am reminded when I see that draft hit my checking account—the most wasted monthly fee I've ever paid—that I am not only a failure at exercise, but at keeping a New Year's resolution.

This past year for me has been one of great change. Growth. This seems to be a pattern in all of life. Make it stop. Or, wait!

Don't, actually!

If things weren't constantly changing, I would be forever bored with life. Wouldn't you?

Many of the past year's changes have been positive and exciting, the evolution of situations that have come to fruition. Things I never saw coming—like this one time I said this one thing (I Ain't Doin' It) and now I have a new life. Kinda like that.

Other changes have been disheartening, disappointing. Some changes, of my own choosing. Other changes, not so much. Relationships ended, hearts divided, sides were taken, judgment, misunderstanding, loss . . . resolve in its own right. Much of the unwelcomed resolve has shaken me to my core and caused me to reevaluate many things that I thought I knew. Resolve that has caused me to have to make my own hard decisions. It's been a painful growth. The loss of a dear relationship this year has also posed many questions that only I could answer.

Who am I?

What do I believe?

Where can I give and bend?

Where can I compromise?

Where can I not?

What have I done?

What have I not?

What can I change?

What can I not?

Some of the answers to these questions are still being decided. Some are crystal clear. Either way, there has been growth in who I am as a woman.

The definition of "growth": Full development; maturity. Evolution.

Wouldn't it be great every now and then if life could just, for five minutes, be perfect—for everything to "be the way it used to be"?

For our babies to stay little, for people who have gone on before us to still be with us, for love that was once given to us to still remain, for friendships that once brought us great comfort and joy to still be intact.

But . . . evolution, growth.

I am learning that the circumstances around me don't have to be perfect and wonderful for growth to occur. Growth is no respecter of persons. If I continue for the next five years to buy my fourteen-year-old a size 14 in clothes, does that stunt his growth? Does he stay the same size 14 because his mom refuses to alter accordingly? Hardly. After a good year, his jeans that once fit will be skintight highwaters in full effect. (Also, he would hate me.) Growth is going to happen whether we like it or not.

In all things, in hard situations, I am continuing to grow—growing as a mother, a friend, a comedienne (when did I even become this?!?), a musician, a writer, a lover of Jesus. I am forever trying to learn to love better, apologize more and judge less, even though so often I miss the mark.

This year I have been pressed on all sides and am seeing what I'm made of. It's beautiful and painful. I'm embarrassed and proud. I'm all of the emotions rolled into one as I see all the facets of the woman I'm becoming. And I'm seeing that some of this growth that was unwelcome has been necessary, and the person I am becoming is far better than the person I was before it came along.

I am grateful for the growth.

And I suck at resolutions, but this year I resolve to

embrace the horrible, wonderful process called growth, because it's coming whether I like it or not. I resolve to not be so easily swayed from others by disappointment or by my own failures, to stand for what is right and know when to bow out gracefully, to submit but never compromise, to speak up more often and know when to say less, to give grace and accept it, to love better, to stay the course and to listen to the beautiful voice of the Lord who wants me close to Him—that voice that is and should always be my ultimate resolve.

The world will always try to dictate who we should be, but I am resolved that only God will decide that for my life. My prayer is that He continues to lead and guide and speak (to that thing in me that wants the sugar) and that I will listen.

This will forever be my New Year's resolution.

If you are trying to quit eating Krispy Kremes or your job or smoking menthols, or you are vowing to go sky-diving or take that trip—godspeed. Don't say you ain't doin' it. You got this. If you don't quite hit your mark, well . . . I promise to be here to help dust you off and keep you moving. I promise to help those around me embrace their growth. We're in this together. Whatever your resolve, know in your knower that you've got what it takes. Go easy on yourself. Love who you are, broken New Year's resolutions and all.

Maybe box jumps just aren't your thing.

CHAPTER 20

I AM DOIN' IT

I'm an idiot. We know this. It's no secret. You see it on the daily, and now, as if that were not enough, it's in written form. For most of my life, the moron seat at the table was reserved for me only in the presence of my close friends and family, but now an extremely large number of people are seeing this nonsense on an up-close-and-personal level. I'm sorry. Or . . . you're welcome. However, you wanna look at it.

I'm a pretty open book. I've never been accused of keeping secrets about myself. I have, however, been accused of being too honest, especially about my own issues. Had I known it could've actually been a job opportunity, I might have started sooner. When I was little, I wanted to be a musician. I dreamed of people from around the world singing the lyrics to my songs with lighters in the air. Instead, people from around the world are quoting what is quite possibly the dumbest, yet most profound, statement to ever come out of my mouth—a statement that rings true in many, if not all, situations of life and can get you out of just about everything you don't wanna do without some deep, two-hour conversation justifying why—I AIN'T DOIN' IT. This one accidental statement has changed the course of my life and hopefully yours, as well. Because now, whatever it is you ain't doin', you get to point to it on the shirt you're wearing and blame it on me. Isn't that awesome?! And make no mistake, I am happy to take one for the team! People don't even ask me stupid questions anymore because they already know what I'm gonna say! And they are correct. Because most things, as you already know, I ain't doin' . . .

See, this is just me. This is my makeup. The content, the personality—it's all real. Nobody writes for me. Nobody coaches me on how to roll my eyes and be sarcastic. I BEEN knowing how to do that.

All. My. Life.

Just ask my parents. And ask my son. I have so beautifully passed this gene down into his entire being. It penetrates his innermost workings to the point that he is incapable of going a full hour without sarcasm pouring from his lips. I'm at about a 70/30 split with him—30 percent completely angry and aggravated, 70 percent extremely proud. But I digress.

My point is this. This is who I am.

I own it. And I love it. I love that I'm doing comedy. I didn't know I would love it as a career, but I do. I love getting to just be me. I don't know how to be anything else, which is probably exactly the reason other things in my life have not worked out so well.

Speaking of things not working out well, after my divorce there were times I wondered how in Lord's name had I gone from vacations and money in the bank to not even knowing if I could afford to buy toothpaste and toilet paper? From never even thinking about turning off a light before I left the house to getting my own place and trying to explain to my daddy why my lights got cut off again? Every day I fought panic and dread. They tried to tie me up and chain me to the nearest table leg at every turn. But peace and contentment were always waiting for me to catch their eye. With a wink and a smile, day after day, they untied my ropes and calmed my fears. They led me out of that dark room and reminded me that it was okay to cry it out and have a come-apart, but that living in a constant state of hysteria was not the life I was called to lead. They offered me the perfect blend of poise and grit, and they waited on me to drink it up and find my center. They were like coffee and fire on the most bitter cold day. They were gifts from the One who loved me most, and I unwrapped them every day like every day was the first time. I thought I would never come out of that season, except that's not entirely true.

My head and my daily circumstances said I wouldn't. My heart and my Heavenly Father said I would—and they were right. I did.

The Lord was well aware of my need for security, and soon made provision. He gave me a job, but not just any job. As I mentioned earlier, through a friend, I came to interview for an administrative position with a company I knew nothing about. I walked in to meet the person who would soon be my boss and dear friend, Andy. He interviewed me and we talked, and I told him my story in true typical fashion: I cried. Folks, this crying-during-interviews thing has got to stop. Seriously.

Anyway, Andy listened. He gave me tissues and coffee and understanding, and he gave me a job. He gave me a salary and benefits, knowing good and well I didn't deserve it. He gave me friendship and family and job security, and he gave me a true glimpse into who Jesus may have been in human form.

During that time, I was finally able to settle in. My job was enjoyable and I looked forward to waking up in the mornings. It was never what I had in mind, but God knew what I needed at that time. He knew that I needed to be surrounded by good people in a sweet space, and He provided. Every day I worked and every day we laughed, and we had meetings and we had worship and prayer, and we lived in an environment of work-done-right. And I was finally on my feet.

Until I wasn't.

For someone who had fought so hard to find stability, in what felt like one fell swoop, I handed it over to a relationship—the one I already told you about—that would end up being my demise. I got tired, but make no mistake, getting tired is no excuse to hand over your dignity and everything you fought for on a silver platter to a toxicity that will devour you like you're a Death Row meal.

I fell deeper and deeper into that black hole of desolation. I traded in my happy, joyful disposition for a life of emptiness. My face no longer lit up. My eyes were hollow and my light was dim as I was single-handedly turning over my life to somebody who was sucking it right out of me. I had never experienced anything like it. I had always considered myself a picture of self-discipline, someone who knew her worth. Full of pride—that's what I was. And now here I was, so addicted to my shameful, septic condition, and I was under so much manipulation that I could not seem to find the door. And many days, I didn't want to find it. My mind was in a constant state of conflict between "everybody just leave me alone" and "somebody please come rescue me." I needed an intervention, and I got one.

I will never forget the feelings of hope and humiliation that cut through my heart, as my fearless leader, for a moment in time, stripped himself of his CEO title and took the ultimate low road of friendship. From the hall-way of my office, he looked at me with love and compassion and guts and resolve and called me out right there in front of God and everybody. He begged me to quit wrecking my life. He pleaded with me to turn the knob and walk out into the light, assuring me that all was not lost—that redemption was available and so were all the people who loved me. And what he did next, his true act of leadership, will forever be branded into my brain. He walked into my office, got on his knees and cried out to God in my place. He spoke for me when I had no words and cried out for me when my tears were gone. His desire to punch me in the throat was superseded by his love for Jesus and for me and our friendship. And he was not the only one. His willingness, and the willingness of count-less other close friends who surrounded me like a herd of elephants during that time, helped guide me out so I could find my way again—so I could find my SELF again. The Karens and Angies and CJs and Tammys—they didn't reprimand me. My church leaders didn't dis-avow me. My family didn't disown me. They loved me until I could love myself.

I didn't immediately see the light. But I knew it was there, and for the first time in a little while, I felt hope. And I knew deep down that God had given me every-thing I needed to step out and make my move. I knew that the love and death of Jesus had paved the road for me, but I would have to walk it, and I was afraid. Afraid of failure. Afraid of relapse. I would be the one to have to take action for my own life, for the choices that I had made and the ones to come, and I knew that if I was ever going to get out, now was the time. Making that first step back into the land of right living was initially a very hard one. It took me a few times of going back and getting a gut-full before I was ready to get gone for good. But I remembered what my granny used to tell me after a breakup: "It won't hurt this bad in a little while." I kept telling myself that until I believed it, and until the continual pouring in of God's word and God's love for me in the form of friends and family covered the wound. I was finally free. The goal now: to stay free.

Looking back, this season of my life has actually done more to shape me into a better person than any good deed or work of service I could've ever done. That strange, awful season of self-loathing, defeat and addiction, if you will, has given me a new perspective on life. Before I chose to go down that rabbit hole, I could only relate to a select few. I couldn't relate to you, addict, until I felt the pull of the dependence so hard that nothing else mattered. I couldn't relate to you, egocentric, until I became selfish and only cared about what made me happy in the moment. I couldn't relate to you either, weakling, until I felt so weak I couldn't even put my own thoughts together. But I see you. And now I know—sometimes it's not as easy as it seems. Sometimes it takes the bosses and the tears and the acts of congress to get us to come to the light. And sometimes the fear of not being able to "stay clean," or the shame or the fear of rejection and not being accepted back into the fold, can be paralyzing. But what's more paralyzing is a life lived in the dark, of half-used potential, of torment and self-inflicted grief. I found, personally, that coming out is worth the grind.

Once I regained my composure and remembered who I was, my good humor and quick wit started making more daily appearances. My mind and my work game were getting strong again, and after a few self-deprecating weeks of forgiving myself for the person I had been, including apologies to my children and those affected by my poor choices, the testimony of a quiet heart and an active determination became more evident in my life to those around me. Actually, "quiet heart" might be a stretch. I wouldn't really classify myself as quiet. My heart, however, had found its resting place in the Lord once again and I was at peace. And that's when the videos hit. And I Ain't Doin' It became a thing. A hilarious, healing thing that kept growing and touching people and making them laugh.

One of my lifelong friends had been in my inner circle—watching and laughing and cheering on this craziness from behind the scenes. I had her on email duty. I worked, she answered. And we read comments. We assessed the situation to see what people were saying and wanting and meaning. And people wanted shirts. Okay, shirts. Surely we could figure out how to make a few (thousand) shirts. That was step one. Done. Now what? Tosha and I talked throughout the days and her voice was like a broken record. And the sentence that she kept repeating had me sick to my stomach with anxiety and excitement and uncertainty.

"They want you to come do comedy."

What did that even mean—do comedy? I wasn't a co-medienne! I was a worship-leader-turned-refinancer. What did I know about stand-up? And who were "they"? Who wanted me to come "do comedy"? On the short list was churches, theaters and casinos. Churches and casi-nos? What in the ever-loving world was happening? Emails poured in, and every day I crunched numbers at my desk and posted videos while Tosha tried to tame the beast. Upon the realization that this was most definitely turning into a thing, we decided it was time for me to come up with a comedy act. An act. I don't even know if I said that right.

My first live performance was in Dallas, Texas. My only job was to open up each session of a women's con-ference for an old friend of mine—two minutes, ten minutes—whatever I wanted it to be. Easy. But not. Tosha and I sat down with a pencil and a piece of scratch paper and started talking nonsense. And we started writing. And there it was—that "Ah ha!" moment of "This is what I'm going to say!" That first night was awful. I was so scared that I cried when it was over. *What am I doing here?!?* Tosh and I got back to our hotel and just sat and stared at each other.

"It was awful wasn't it?" I asked. "It wasn't great . . ." she said. My head hung, but then she said something that spurred me on for the long haul.

". . . but you were made for this. It may not have been great but it was beautiful, and it's in you and they love you and you are doin' it . . . I know you're scared, but do it afraid. You were made for this."

I don't really know if she said "you are doin' it," but it sounded right. Either way, it was what I needed to hear. And somewhere in my gut, I knew she was right. It was awful, and so very weird . . . but it was in me.

After we returned home, numbers kept going up and emails kept pouring in and I had a decision to make. I was at a point where I could no longer devote my whole self to my job and give this new thing, whatever it was, any attention. The thought of giving up the stability that God had provided for me with my current setup and trading it in for the unknown scared the crap out of me. At the end of the day, though, I could not rest until I had seen about it. I could not let the ship sail without taking it for a test run. Call it what you want—curiosity, fear of missing out. I call it God. But how? *How, God, can you,*

after all I've just done and been through and come out of,
bless me with this new thing? He's funny that way, isn't
He? There was an obvious thing happening, and I could
either pretend it wasn't or jump in with both feet. So I
jumped. And I am so glad I did.

I hated leaving work and Andy and his wife and all
my people, but I knew that I had to scratch this itch and
that even if I failed, at least I could say I tried. How many
more times is the opportunity going to come around for
me to run straight through this many open doors at
once? Maybe never.

So, once again, I packed up my kids and headed three
hours east to Nashville. And once again, more transition.
And more of that thing that tries to hold me hostage:
Fear. Fear of the unknown. Fear of forward movement
and the things I can't control. Isn't it funny how the Lord
can lay the most beautiful thing in front of us, but sometimes we just don't know how to embrace it? Maybe it's
just me.

I have found during this process that, sadly, even as a
comedienne, I don't always know how to enjoy life, even
in the sweet spot.

I watch everybody else enjoy life and seize their opportunities and I stand to the side because I feel unde-
serving or I feel the weight. I feel the guilt and the fear,
and I forget that I don't have to have all the answers and
all the control. It's okay to say, "You know what? I don't

know what's coming next, but God does and that is enough." I forget the goodness of the Lord because I get so wrapped up in my own condemnation from my past. I sit and I try to figure out how and why in the world God would wait until my greatest failure to give me this gift, but isn't that the answer? I had to go through the transitions and the questions and the divorce and the moral failure to get here. I had to get to that place where I knew that I didn't do this. He did. I didn't know I was even capable, but He did.

And He knows best. He knows the way that I take and He can see around every corner.

I see transition, but He sees promise.

I see fear of the unknown. He sees fun and excitement.

I see difficulty. He sees another opportunity to show me His faithfulness.

I'm learning. To stop and smell the roses, to enjoy the ride, run the field.

If we don't, we might be missing the greatest game ever.

I don't wanna miss the fun, y'all.

I wanna walk in the joy and the goodness and run in the freedom that comes with trusting God. We belong to Jesus. We don't have all the answers, but He does.

So far, this thing called comedy—I AM DOIN' IT! And I'm trying my hand at a few other things I didn't know I could do, either. I'm writing and playing music and traveling, and I'm still doing my favorite thing of all—motherhood. And I'm messing up left and right. Some days it's one step forward and two steps back, but I'm present. And I'm enjoying the ride, because I'm finally figuring out that my life and my direction and my future, it all belongs to Somebody who has way more answers than I do. And He gives me the courage to do it— whatever "IT" is. Guilt free. I'm learning that my mistakes don't disqualify me from a life full of fun and excitement. I'm learning that I am not defined by my past. I'm learning to live lighthearted—to laugh at myself (and you) and not take myself so seriously. Life is too short. We are all full of greatness and accomplishments— missteps and failures. We are all a little weird and a little crazy. At times we are scared and we are weak. But we are also bold and courageous. Stronger than we know and more capable than we can imagine. We have what it takes to do the thing—to forgive, to show humility, to be brave, to fight for the underdog, to stand up for justice. We have what it takes to work the job and get the lights turned back on. To walk through divorce and loss. To take a seat when it's time to let somebody else shine, but stand tall when it's our turn on stage.

Whatever that thing is that you're scared of, stand toe to toe and do it afraid. Hold that mic and tell that joke and when nobody laughs, go home and cry and get back up and tell it a different way tomorrow. When that breakup comes, tell yourself hurt doesn't last forever and that you're going to be okay. When you fail as a parent or an employee or a friend, show humility, right your wrong and keep it moving. Your failure isn't your future. The Giver of All Good Things has a door with your name on it. And He's going to open it and walk you through it at just the right time. It may be tomorrow. It may be after your greatest failure. Whenever it opens, walk through it head up and chest out. Tell the dread that you ain't doin' it, but look that road that lies ahead square in the face and tell it that you are. And then walk it.

Because I am.

I am doin' it.

ACKNOWLEDGMENTS

*T*he trickiest and perhaps most difficult portion of this book to write was the acknowledgments. I'll start by saying this—so many of you have contributed to the writing of this book in some way, shape or form. Many of you laid eyes on the pages throughout the editing process, offering encouragement, laughter, tears and constructive criticism along the way. Some of you have contributed to its creative content, whether with thoughts and ideas or because you were literally part of an actual story. But all of you who have walked with me through the making of this book have offered sincere belief in my ability to create this writing, and you have fortified my resolve to unashamedly throw it to the masses. To each and every one of you, my deepest gratitude.

There are a few people whom I have developed sincere relationships with strictly through the development of this book and the ones to come:

Lisa Jackson—literary agent and friend. I knew Lisa was for me the first time I ever talked to her. She not only sought me out and introduced me to the world of publishing, but she has continued to remind me along the way that I am playing on a field that I deserve to be on. She convinced me that I'm a writer and that I have something to say. She fought for me with honesty and integrity and believed the best in me and my written word. You may never be so inclined to write, much less publish, a book, but you most definitely need a Lisa Jackson in your life.

Becky Nesbitt—book editor and constant reader of all my words. Her kind and genuine personality made me do a double take, but it was her passion and belief in my writings that she had already digested into her system that made me sign on the dotted line. She has listened and understood my heart. She has tightened and honed my words without losing grit or meaning. She has helped me understand how to hear my readers and communicate my words in effective ways without compromise. Most importantly, she believes that humor is medicinal and that the way I impart it matters.

Simon & Schuster and Howard Books—thank you to one of the Big Five for taking a chance on me. You're a risky bunch and I love you for it.

Thank you, once again, to each and every one of you who have made this book come to life, and to every person who has helped shape me into the woman I am today. I am forever grateful.